Arthur M⬛⬛⬛ the Uni-
versity of⬛⬛⬛ Salesman
(1949), ⬛⬛⬛ y of Two
Mondays ⬛⬛⬛ ce (1968),
The Creation of the World and Other Business (1972), and The American Clock
(1980). He has also written two novels, Focus (1945) and The Misfits, which
was filmed in 1960, and the text for In Russia (1969), Chinese Encounters
(1979), and In the Country (1977), three books of photographs by his wife,
Inge Morath. His most recent works include a memoir, Timebends (1987),
and the plays The Ride Down Mt. Morgan (1991), The Last Yankee (1993),
Broken Glass (1993), which won the 1995 Olivier Award for Best Play of
the London Season, and Mr. Peters' Connections (1998). He has twice won the
New York Drama Critics Circle Award, and in 1949 he was awarded the
Pulitzer Prize.

BY ARTHUR MILLER

DRAMA
The Golden Years
The Man Who Had All the Luck
All My Sons
Death of a Salesman
An Enemy of the People (*adaptation of the play by Ibsen*)
The Crucible
A View from the Bridge
After the Fall
Incident at Vichy
The Price
The American Clock
The Creation of the World and Other Business
The Archbishop's Ceiling
The Ride Down Mt. Morgan
Broken Glass
Mr. Peters' Connections

ONE-ACT PLAYS
A View from the Bridge, *one-act version, with* A Memory of Two Mondays
Elegy for a Lady (*in* Two-Way Mirror)
Some Kind of Love Story (*in* Two-Way Mirror)
I Can't Remember Anything (*in* Danger: Memory!)
Clara (*in* Danger: Memory!)
The Last Yankee

OTHER WORKS
Situation Normal
The Misfits (*a cinema novel*)
Focus (*a novel*)
I Don't Need You Anymore (*short stories*)
In the Country (*reportage with Inge Morath photographs*)
Chinese Encounters (*reportage with Inge Morath photographs*)
In Russia (*reportage with Inge Morath photographs*)
Salesman in Beijing (*a memoir*)
Timebends (*autobiography*)
Homely Girl, A Life (*novella*)

COLLECTIONS
Arthur Miller's Collected Plays (Volumes I and II)
The Portable Arthur Miller
The Theater Essays of Arthur Miller (*Robert Martin, editor*)

VIKING CRITICAL LIBRARY EDITIONS
Death of a Salesman (*edited by Gerald Weales*)
The Crucible (*edited by Gerald Weales*)

TELEVISION WORKS
Playing for Time

SCREENPLAYS
The Misfits
Everybody Wins
The Crucible

Broken Glass
A Play in Two Acts

ARTHUR MILLER

PENGUIN BOOKS

To Inge Morath

PENGUIN BOOKS
Published by the Penguin Group
Penguin Books USA Inc., 375 Hudson Street, New York, New York 10014, U.S.A.
Penguin Books Ltd, 27 Wrights Lane, London W8 5TZ, England
Penguin Books Australia Ltd, Ringwood, Victoria, Australia
Penguin Books Canada Ltd, 10 Alcorn Avenue,
Toronto, Ontario, Canada M4V 3B2
Penguin Books (N.Z.) Ltd, 182–190 Wairau Road,
Auckland 10, New Zealand

Penguin Books Ltd, Registered Offices: Harmondsworth, Middlesex, England

First published in Penguin Books 1994

9   10

Library of Congress Cataloging in Publication Data
Miller, Arthur.
Broken glass : a play / by Arthur Miller.
p.   cm.
ISBN 0 14 02.4938 9
1. Holocaust, Jewish (1939–1945)—Foreign public opinion,
American—Drama.   2. Jewish men—New York (N.Y.)—Drama.
3. Marriage—New York (N.Y.)—Drama.   4. Bankers—New York (N.Y.)—
Drama.   I. Title.
PS3525.I5156B76   1994

812'.52—dc20   93-20949

Printed in the United States of America
Set in Bembo

*The play takes place in Brooklyn in the last days
of November 1938, in the office of
Dr. Harry Hyman, the bedroom of the Gellburg
house, and the office of Stanton Case.*

CAST OF CHARACTERS

Phillip Gellburg	Ron Rifkin
Sylvia Gellburg	Amy Irving
Dr. Harry Hyman	David Dukes
Margaret Hyman	Frances Conroy
Harriet	Lauren Klein
Stanton Case	George N. Martin

Directed by John Tillinger

The original production was staged at the
Long Wharf Theater in New Haven,
Connecticut.

Final Acting Version

Act One

SCENE ONE

*A lone cellist is discovered, playing a simple tune.
The tune finishes. Light goes out on the cellist and
rises on. . . .*

*Office of Dr. Harry Hyman in his home. Alone on
stage Phillip Gellburg, an intense man in his late
forties, waits in perfect stillness, legs crossed. He is
in a black suit, black tie and shoes, and white shirt.*

*Margaret Hyman, the doctor's wife, enters. She is
lusty, energetic, carrying pruning shears.*

MARGARET: He'll be right with you, he's just changing. Can
I get you something? Tea?

GELLBURG, *faint reprimand:* He said seven o'clock sharp.

MARGARET: He was held up in the hospital, that new
union's pulled a strike, imagine? A strike in a hospital? It's
incredible. And his horse went lame.

GELLBURG: His horse?

MARGARET: He rides on Ocean Parkway every afternoon.

GELLBURG, *attempting easy familiarity:* Oh yes, I heard about that . . . it's very nice. You're Mrs. Hyman?

MARGARET: I've nodded to you on the street for years now, but you're too preoccupied to notice.

GELLBURG, *a barely hidden boast:* Lot on my mind, usually. *A certain amused loftiness.*—So you're his nurse, too.

MARGARET: We met in Mount Sinai when he was interning. He's lived to regret it. *She laughs in a burst.*

GELLBURG: That's some laugh you've got there. I sometimes hear you all the way down the block to my house.

MARGARET: Can't help it, my whole family does it. I'm originally from Minnesota. It's nice to meet you finally, Mr. Goldberg.

GELLBURG: —It's Gellburg, not Goldberg.

MARGARET: Oh, I'm sorry.

GELLBURG: G-e-l-l-b-u-r-g. It's the only one in the phone book.

MARGARET: It does sound like Goldberg.

GELLBURG: But it's not, it's Gellburg. *A distinction.* We're from Finland originally.

MARGARET: Oh! We came from Lithuania . . . Kazauskis?

GELLBURG, *put down momentarily:* Don't say.

MARGARET, *trying to charm him to his ease:* Ever been to Minnesota?

GELLBURG: New York State's the size of France, what would I go to Minnesota for?

MARGARET: Nothing. Just there's a lot of Finns there.

GELLBURG: Well there's Finns all over.

MARGARET, *defeated, shows the clipper:* . . . I'll get back to my roses. Whatever it is, I hope you'll be feeling better.

GELLBURG: It's not me.

MARGARET: Oh. 'Cause you seem a little pale.

GELLBURG: Me?—I'm always this color. It's my wife.

MARGARET: I'm sorry to hear that, she's a lovely woman. It's nothing serious, is it?

GELLBURG: He's just had a specialist put her through some tests, I'm waiting to hear. I think it's got him mystified.

MARGARET: Well, I mustn't butt in. *Makes to leave but can't resist.* Can you say what it is?

GELLBURG: She can't walk.

MARGARET: What do you mean?

GELLBURG, *an overtone of protest of some personal victimization:*
Can't stand up. No feeling in her legs.—I'm sure it'll pass,
but it's terrible.

MARGARET: But I only saw her in the grocery . . . can't be
more than ten days ago . . .

GELLBURG: It's nine days today.

MARGARET: But she's such a wonderful-looking woman.
Does she have fever?

GELLBURG: No.

MARGARET: Thank God, then it's not polio.

GELLBURG: No, she's in perfect health otherwise.

MARGARET: Well Harry'll get to the bottom of it if anybody
can. They call him from everywhere for opinions, you
know . . . Boston, Chicago . . . By rights he ought to be
on Park Avenue if he only had the ambition, but he always wanted a neighborhood practice. Why, I don't
know—we never invite anybody, we never go out, all
our friends are in Manhattan. But it's his nature, you can't
fight a person's nature. Like me for instance, I like to talk
and I like to laugh. You're not much of a talker, are you.

GELLBURG, *a purse-mouthed smile:* When I can get a word in edgewise.

MARGARET, *burst of laughter:* Ha!—so you've got a sense of humor after all. Well give my best to Mrs. Goldberg.

GELLBURG: Gellbu . . .

MARGARET, *hits her own head:* Gellburg, excuse me! —It practically sounds like Goldberg . . .

GELLBURG: No-no, look in the phone book, it's the only one, G-e-l-l . . .

Enter Dr. Hyman.

MARGARET, *with a little wave to Gellburg:* Be seeing you!

GELLBURG: Be in good health.

Margaret exits.

HYMAN, *in his early fifties, a healthy, rather handsome man, a determined scientific idealist. Settling behind his desk—chuckling:* She chew your ear off?

GELLBURG, *his worldly mode:* Not too bad, I've had worse.

HYMAN: Well there's no way around it, women are talkers . . . *Grinning familiarly:* But try living without them, right?

GELLBURG: Without women?

HYMAN, *he sees Gellburg has flushed; there is a short hiatus, then:*
. . . Well, never mind. —I'm glad you could make it
tonight, I wanted to talk to you before I see your wife
again tomorrow. *Opens cigar humidor.* Smoke?

GELLBURG: No thanks, never have. Isn't it bad for you?

HYMAN: Certainly is. *Lights a cigar.* But more people die of
rat bite, you know.

GELLBURG: Rat bite!

HYMAN: Oh yes, but they're mostly the poor so it's not an
interesting statistic. Have you seen her tonight or did you
come here from the office?

GELLBURG: I thought I'd see you before I went home.
But I phoned her this afternoon—same thing, no
change.

HYMAN: How's she doing with the wheelchair?

GELLBURG: Better, she can get herself in and out of the
bed now.

HYMAN: Good. And she manages the bathroom?

GELLBURG: Oh yes. I got the maid to come in the mornings
to help her take a bath, clean up . . .

HYMAN: Good. Your wife has a lot of courage, I admire that kind of woman. My wife is similar; I like the type.

GELLBURG: What type you mean?

HYMAN: You know—vigorous. I mean mentally and . . . you know, just generally. Moxie.

GELLBURG: Oh.

HYMAN: Forget it, it was only a remark.

GELLBURG: No, you're right, I never thought of it, but she is unusually that way.

HYMAN, *pause, some prickliness here which he can't understand:* Doctor Sherman's report . . .

GELLBURG: What's he say?

HYMAN: I'm getting to it.

GELLBURG: Oh. Beg your pardon.

HYMAN: You'll have to bear with me . . . may I call you Phillip?

GELLBURG: Certainly.

HYMAN: I don't express my thoughts very quickly, Phillip.

GELLBURG: Likewise. Go ahead, take your time.

HYMAN: People tend to overestimate the wisdom of physicians so I try to think things through before I speak to a patient.

GELLBURG: I'm glad to hear that.

HYMAN: Aesculapius stuttered, you know—ancient Greek god of medicine. But probably based on a real physician who hesitated about giving advice. Somerset Maugham stammered, studied medicine. Anton Chekhov, great writer, also a doctor, had tuberculosis. Doctors are very often physically defective in some way, that's why they're interested in healing.

GELLBURG, *impressed:* I see.

HYMAN, *pause, thinks:* I find this Adolf Hitler very disturbing. You been following him in the papers?

GELLBURG: Well yes, but not much. My average day in the office is ten, eleven hours.

HYMAN: They've been smashing the Jewish stores in Berlin all week, you know.

GELLBURG: Oh yes, I saw that again yesterday.

HYMAN: Very disturbing. Forcing old men to scrub the sidewalks with toothbrushes. On the Kurfürstendamm, that's equivalent to Fifth Avenue. Nothing but hoodlums in uniform.

GELLBURG: My wife is very upset about that.

HYMAN: I know, that's why I mention it. *Hesitates*. And how about you?

GELLBURG: Of course. It's a terrible thing. Why do you ask?

HYMAN, *a smile:* —I don't know, I got the feeling she may be afraid she's annoying you when she talks about such things.

GELLBURG: Why? I don't mind. —She said she's annoying me?

HYMAN: Not in so many words, but . . .

GELLBURG: I can't believe she'd say a thing like . . .

HYMAN: Wait a minute, I didn't say she said it . . .

GELLBURG: She doesn't annoy me, but what can be done about such things? The thing is, she doesn't like to hear about the other side of it.

HYMAN: What other side?

GELLBURG: It's no excuse for what's happening over there, but German Jews can be pretty . . . you know . . . *Pushes up his nose with his forefinger.* Not that they're pushy like the ones from Poland or Russia but a friend of mine's in the garment industry; these German Jews won't take an ordinary good job, you know; it's got to be pretty high up in the firm or they're insulted. And they can't even speak English.

HYMAN: Well I guess a lot of them were pretty important over there.

GELLBURG: I know, but they're supposed to be *refugees*, aren't they? With all our unemployment you'd think they'd appreciate a little more. Latest official figure is twelve million unemployed you know, and it's probably bigger but Roosevelt can't admit it, after the fortune he's pouring into WPA and the rest of that welfare *mishugas*. —But she's not *annoying* me, for God's sake.

HYMAN: . . . I just thought I'd mention it; but it was only a feeling I had . . .

GELLBURG: I'll tell you right now, I don't run with the crowd, I see with these eyes, nobody else's.

HYMAN: I see that. —You're very unusual— *Grinning.* — you almost sound like a Republican.

GELLBURG: Why?—the Torah says a Jew has to be a Democrat? I didn't get where I am by agreeing with everybody.

HYMAN: Well that's a good thing; you're independent. *Nods, puffs.* You know, what mystifies me is that the Germans I knew in Heidelberg . . . I took my M.D. there . . .

GELLBURG: You got along with them.

HYMAN: Some of the finest people I ever met.

GELLBURG: Well there you go.

HYMAN: We had a marvelous student choral group, fantastic voices; Saturday nights, we'd have a few beers and go singing through the streets. . . . People'd applaud from the windows.

GELLBURG: Don't say.

HYMAN: I simply can't imagine those people marching into Austria, and now they say Czechoslovakia's next, and Poland. . . . But fanatics have taken Germany, I guess, and they can be brutal, you know . . .

GELLBURG: Listen, I sympathize with these refugees, but . . .

HYMAN, *cutting him off:* I had quite a long talk with Sylvia yesterday, I suppose she told you?

GELLBURG, *a tensing:* Well . . . no, she didn't mention. What about?

HYMAN, *surprised by Sylvia's omission:* . . . Well about her condition, and . . . just in passing . . . your relationship.

GELLBURG, *flushing:* My relationship?

HYMAN: . . . It was just in passing.

GELLBURG: Why, what'd she say?

HYMAN: Well that you . . . get along very well.

GELLBURG: Oh.

HYMAN, *encouragingly, as he sees Gellburg's small tension:* I found her a remarkably well-informed woman. Especially for this neighborhood.

GELLBURG, *a pridefully approving nod; relieved that he can speak of her positively:* That's practically why we got together in the first place. I don't exaggerate, if Sylvia was a man she could have run the Federal Reserve. You could talk to Sylvia like you talk to a man.

HYMAN: I'll bet.

GELLBURG, *a purse-mouthed grin:* . . . Not that talking was all we did—but you turn your back on Sylvia and she's got her nose in a book or a magazine. I mean there's not one woman in ten around here could even tell you who their Congressman is. And you can throw in the men, too. *Pause.* So where are we?

HYMAN: Doctor Sherman confirms my diagnosis. I ask you to listen carefully, will you?

GELLBURG, *brought up:* Of course, that's why I came.

HYMAN: We can find no physical reason for her inability to walk.

GELLBURG: No physical reason . . .

HYMAN: We are almost certain that this is a psychological condition.

GELLBURG: But she's numb, she has no feeling in her legs.

HYMAN: Yes. This is what we call an hysterical paralysis. Hysterical doesn't mean she screams and yells . . .

GELLBURG: Oh, I know. It means like . . . ah . . . *Bumbles off.*

HYMAN, *a flash of umbrage, dislike:* Let me explain what it means, okay?—Hysteria comes from the Greek word for the womb because it was thought to be a symptom of female anxiety. Of course it isn't, but that's where it comes from. People who are anxious enough or really frightened can imagine they've gone blind or deaf, for instance . . . and they really can't see or hear. It was sometimes called shell-shock during the War.

GELLBURG: You mean . . . you don't mean she's . . . crazy.

HYMAN: We'll have to talk turkey, Phillip. If I'm going to do you any good I'm going to have to ask you some personal questions. Some of them may sound raw, but I've only been superficially acquainted with Sylvia's family and I need to know more . . .

GELLBURG: She says you treated her father . . .

HYMAN: Briefly; a few visits shortly before he passed away. They're fine people. I hate like hell to see this happen to her, you see what I mean?

GELLBURG: You can tell it to me; is she crazy?

HYMAN: Phillip, are you? Am I? In one way or another, who isn't crazy? The main difference is that our kind of crazy still allows us to walk around and tend to our business. But who knows?—people like us may be the craziest of all.

GELLBURG, *scoffing grin:* Why!

HYMAN: Because we don't know we're nuts, and the other kind does.

GELLBURG: I don't know about that . . .

HYMAN: Well, it's neither here nor there.

GELLBURG: I certainly don't think *I'm* nuts.

HYMAN: I wasn't saying that . . .

GELLBURG: What do you mean, then?

HYMAN, *grinning:* You're not an easy man to talk to, are you.

GELLBURG: Why? If I don't understand I have to ask, don't I?

HYMAN: Yes, you're right.

GELLBURG: That's the way I am—they don't pay me for being easy to talk to.

HYMAN: You're in . . . real estate?

GELLBURG: I'm head of the Mortgage Department of Brooklyn Guarantee and Trust.

HYMAN: Oh, that's right, she told me.

GELLBURG: We are the largest lender east of the Mississippi.

HYMAN: Really. *Fighting deflation.* Well, let me tell you my approach; if possible I'd like to keep her out of that whole psychiatry rigmarole. Not that I'm against it, but I think you get further faster, sometimes, with a little common sense and some plain human sympathy. Can we talk turkey? *Tuchas offen tisch,* you know any Yiddish?

GELLBURG: Yes, it means get your ass on the table.

HYMAN: Correct. So let's forget crazy and try to face the facts. We have a strong, healthy woman who has no physical ailment, and suddenly can't stand on her legs. Why?

He goes silent. Gellburg shifts uneasily.

I don't mean to embarrass you . . .

GELLBURG, *an angry smile:* You're not embarrassing me. — What do you want to know?

HYMAN, *sets himself, then launches:* In these cases there is often a sexual disability. You have relations, I imagine?

GELLBURG: Relations? Yes, we have relations.

HYMAN, *a softening smile:* Often?

GELLBURG: What's that got to do with it?

HYMAN: Sex could be connected. You don't have to answer . . .

GELLBURG: No-no it's all right. . . . I would say it depends—maybe twice, three times a week.

HYMAN, *seems surprised:* Well that's good. She seems satisfied?

GELLBURG, *shrugs; hostilely:* I guess she is, sure.

HYMAN: That was a foolish question, forget it.

GELLBURG, *flushed:* Why, did she mention something about this?

HYMAN: Oh no, it's just something I thought of later.

GELLBURG: Well, I'm no Rudolph Valentino but I . . .

HYMAN: Rudolph Valentino probably wasn't either.—What about before she collapsed; was that completely out of the blue or . . .

GELLBURG, *relieved to be off the other subject:* I tell you, looking back I wonder if something happened when they started putting all the pictures in the paper. About these Nazi carryings-on. I noticed she started . . . staring at them . . . in a very peculiar way. And . . . I don't know. I think it made her angry or something.

HYMAN: At you.

GELLBURG: Well . . . *Nods, agreeing.* In general. —Personally I don't think they should be publishing those kind of pictures.

HYMAN: Why not?

GELLBURG: She scares herself to death with them—three thousand miles away, and what does it accomplish! Except maybe put some fancy new ideas into these anti-Semites walking around New York here.

Slight pause.

HYMAN: Tell me how she collapsed. You were going to the movies . . . ?

GELLBURG, *breathing more deeply:* Yes. We were just starting down the porch steps and all of a sudden her . . . *Difficulty; he breaks off.*

HYMAN: I'm sorry but I . . .

GELLBURG: . . . Her legs turned to butter. I couldn't stand her up. Kept falling around like a rag doll. I had to carry her into the house. And she kept apologizing . . . ! *He weeps; recovers.* I can't talk about it.

HYMAN: It's all right.

GELLBURG: She's always been such a level-headed woman. *Weeping threatens again.* I don't know what to do. She's my life.

HYMAN: I'll do my best for her, Phillip, she's a wonderful woman. —Let's talk about something else. What do you do exactly?

GELLBURG: I mainly evaluate properties.

HYMAN: Whether to grant a mortgage . . .

GELLBURG: And how big a one and the terms.

HYMAN: How's the Depression hit you?

GELLBURG: Well, it's no comparison with '32 to '36, let's say—we were foreclosing left and right in those days. But we're on our feet and running.

HYMAN: And you head the department . . .

GELLBURG: Above me is only Mr. Case. Stanton Wylie Case; he's chairman and president. You're not interested in boat racing.

HYMAN: Why?

GELLBURG: His yacht won the America's Cup two years ago. For the second time. The *Aurora*?

HYMAN: Oh yes! I think I read about . . .

GELLBURG: He's had me aboard twice.

HYMAN: Really.

GELLBURG, *the grin:* The only Jew ever set foot on that deck.

HYMAN: Don't say.

GELLBURG: In fact, I'm the only Jew ever worked for Brooklyn Guarantee in their whole history.

HYMAN: That so.

GELLBURG: Oh yes. And they go back to the 1890s. Started right out of accountancy school and moved straight up. They've been wonderful to me; it's a great firm.

> *A long moment as Hyman stares at Gellburg, who is proudly positioned now, absorbing his poise from the evoked memories of his success. Gradually Gellburg turns to him.*

How could this be a mental condition?

HYMAN: It's unconscious; like . . . well take yourself; I notice you're all in black. Can I ask you why?

GELLBURG: I've worn black since high school.

HYMAN: No particular reason.

GELLBURG, *shrugs:* Always liked it, that's all.

HYMAN: Well it's a similar thing with her; she doesn't know why she's doing this, but some very deep, hidden part of her mind is directing her to do it. You don't agree.

GELLBURG: I don't know.

HYMAN: You think she knows what she's doing?

GELLBURG: Well I always liked black for business reasons.

HYMAN: It gives you authority?

GELLBURG: Not exactly authority, but I wanted to look a little older. See, I graduated high school at fifteen and I was only twenty-two when I entered the firm. But I knew what I was doing.

HYMAN: Then you think she's doing this on purpose?

GELLBURG:—Except she's numb; nobody can purposely do that, can they?

HYMAN: I don't think so. —I tell you, Phillip, not really knowing your wife, if you have any idea why she could be doing this to herself . . .

GELLBURG: I told you, I don't know.

HYMAN: Nothing occurs to you.

GELLBURG, *an edge of irritation:* I can't think of anything.

HYMAN: I tell you a funny thing, talking to her, she doesn't seem all that unhappy.

GELLBURG: Say!—yes, that's what I mean. That's exactly what I mean. It's like she's almost . . . I don't know . . . enjoying herself. I mean in a way.

HYMAN: How could that be possible?

GELLBURG: Of course she apologizes for it, and for making it hard for me—you know, like I have to do a lot of the cooking now, and tending to my laundry and so on . . . I even shop for groceries and the butcher . . . and change the sheets . . .

> *He breaks off with some realization. Hyman doesn't speak. A long pause.*

You mean . . . she's doing it against me?

HYMAN: I don't know, what do *you* think?

> *Stares for a long moment, then makes to rise, obviously deeply disturbed.*

GELLBURG: I'd better be getting home. *Lost in his own thought.* I don't know whether to ask you this or not.

HYMAN: What's to lose, go ahead.

GELLBURG: My parents were from the old country, you know,—I don't know if it was in Poland someplace or Russia—but there was this woman who they say was . . .

you know . . . gotten into by a . . . like the ghost of a dead person . . .

HYMAN: A dybbuk.

GELLBURG: That's it. And it made her lose her mind and so forth. —You believe in that? They had to get a rabbi to pray it out of her body. But you think that's possible?

HYMAN: Do I think so? No. Do you?

GELLBURG: Oh no. It just crossed my mind.

HYMAN: Well I wouldn't know how to pray it out of her, so . . .

GELLBURG: Be straight with me—is she going to come out of this?

HYMAN: Well, let's talk again after I see her tomorrow. Maybe I should tell you . . . I have this unconventional approach to illness, Phillip. Especially where the mental element is involved. I believe we get sick in twos and threes and fours, not alone as individuals. You follow me? I want you to do me a favor, will you?

GELLBURG: What's that.

HYMAN: You won't be offended, okay?

GELLBURG, *tensely:* Why should I be offended?

HYMAN: I'd like you to give her a lot of loving. *Fixing Gellburg in his gaze.* Can you? It's important now.

GELLBURG: Say, you're not blaming this on me, are you?

HYMAN: What's the good of blame? —from here on out, *tuchas offen tisch,* okay? And Phillip?

GELLBURG: Yes?

HYMAN, *a light chuckle:* Try not to let yourself get mad.

> *Gellburg turns and goes out. Hyman returns to his desk, makes some notes. Margaret enters.*

MARGARET: That's one miserable little pisser.

> *He writes, doesn't look up.*

He's a dictator, you know. I was just remembering when I went to the grandmother's funeral? He stands outside the funeral parlor and decides who's going to sit with who in the limousines for the cemetery. "You sit with him, you sit with her . . ." And they obey him like he owned the funeral!

HYMAN: Did you find out what's playing?

MARGARET: At the Beverly they've got Ginger Rogers and Fred Astaire. Jimmy Cagney's at the Rialto but it's another gangster story.

HYMAN: I have a sour feeling about this thing. I barely know my way around psychiatry. I'm not completely sure I ought to get into it.

MARGARET: Why not?—She's a very beautiful woman.

HYMAN, *matching her wryness:* Well, is that a reason to turn her away? *He laughs, grasps her hand.* Something about it fascinates me—no disease and she's paralyzed. I'd really love to give it a try. I mean I don't want to turn myself into a post office, shipping all the hard cases to specialists, the woman's sick and I'd like to help.

MARGARET: But if you're not getting anywhere in a little while you'll promise to send her to somebody.

HYMAN: Absolutely. *Committed now: full enthusiasm.* I just feel there's something about it that I understand.—Let's see Cagney.

MARGARET: Oh, no Fred Astaire.

HYMAN: That's what I meant. Come here.

MARGARET, *as he embraces her:* We should leave now . . .

HYMAN: You're the best, Margaret.

MARGARET: A lot of good it does me.

HYMAN: If it really bothers you I'll get someone else to take the case.

MARGARET: You won't, you know you won't.

He is lifting her skirt

Don't, Harry. Come on.

She frees her skirt, he kisses her breasts.

HYMAN: Should I tell you what I'd like to do with you?

MARGARET: Tell me, yes, tell me. And make it wonderful.

HYMAN: We find an island and we strip and go riding on this white horse . . .

MARGARET: Together.

HYMAN: You in front.

MARGARET: Naturally.

HYMAN: And then we go swimming . . .

MARGARET: Harry, that's lovely.

HYMAN: And I hire this shark to swim very close and we just manage to get out of the water, and we're so grateful to be alive we fall down on the beach together and . . .

MARGARET, *pressing his lips shut:* Sometimes you're so good. *She kisses him.*

Blackout.

SCENE TWO

The Lone Cellist plays. Then lights go down . . .

Next evening. The Gellburg bedroom. Sylvia Gell-burg is seated in a wheelchair reading a newspaper. She is in her mid-forties, a buxom, capable, and warm woman. Right now her hair is brushed down to her shoulders, and she is in a nightgown and robe.

She reads the paper with an intense, almost haunted interest, looking up now and then to visualize.

Her sister Harriet, a couple of years younger, is straightening up the bedcover.

HARRIET: So what do you want, steak or chicken? Or maybe he'd like chops for a change.

SYLVIA: Please, don't put yourself out, Phillip doesn't mind a little shopping.

HARRIET: What's the matter with you, I'm going anyway, he's got enough on his mind.

SYLVIA: Well all right, get a couple of chops.

HARRIET: And what about you. You have to start eating!

SYLVIA: I'm eating.

HARRIET: What, a piece of cucumber? Look how pale you are. And what is this with newspapers night and day?

SYLVIA: I like to see what's happening.

HARRIET: I don't know about this doctor. Maybe you need a specialist.

SYLVIA: He brought one two days ago, Doctor Sherman. From Mount Sinai.

HARRIET: Really? And?

SYLVIA: We're waiting to hear. I like Doctor Hyman.

HARRIET: Nobody in the family ever had anything like this. You feel *something*, though, don't you?

SYLVIA, *pause, she lifts her face:* Yes . . . but inside, not on the skin. *Looks at her legs.* I can harden the muscles but I can't lift them. *Strokes her thighs.* I seem to have an ache. Not only here but . . . *She runs her hands down her trunk.* My whole body seems . . . I can't describe it. It's like I was just born and I . . . didn't want to come out yet. Like a deep, terrible aching . . .

HARRIET: Didn't want to come out yet! What are you talking about?

SYLVIA, *sighs gently, knowing Harriet can never understand:* Maybe if he has a nice duck. If not, get the chops. And thanks, Harriet, it's sweet of you.—By the way, what did David decide?

HARRIET: He's not going to college.

SYLVIA, *shocked:* I don't believe it! With a scholarship and he's not going?

HARRIET: What can we do? *Resignedly.* He says college wouldn't help him get a job anyway.

SYLVIA: Harriet, that's terrible!—Listen, tell him I have to talk to him.

HARRIET: Would you! I was going to ask you but with this happening. *Indicates her legs.* I didn't think you'd . . .

SYLVIA: Never mind, tell him to come over. And you must tell Murray he's got to put his foot down—you've got a brilliant boy! My God . . . *Picks up the newspaper.* If I'd had a chance to go to college I'd have had a whole different life, you can't let this happen.

HARRIET: I'll tell David . . . I wish I knew what is suddenly so interesting in a newspaper. This is not normal, Sylvia, is it?

SYLVIA, *pause, she stares ahead:* They are making old men crawl around and clean the sidewalks with toothbrushes.

HARRIET: Who is?

SYLVIA: In Germany. Old men with beards!

HARRIET: So why are you so interested in that? What business of yours is that?

SYLVIA, *slight pause; searches within:* I don't really know. *A slight pause.* Remember Grandpa? His eyeglasses with the bent sidepiece? One of the old men in the paper was his spitting image, he had the same exact glasses with the wire frames. I can't get it out of my mind. On their knees on the sidewalk, two old men. And there's fifteen or twenty people standing in a circle laughing at them scrubbing with toothbrushes. There's three women in the picture; they're holding their coat collars closed, so it must have been cold . . .

HARRIET: Why would they make them scrub with toothbrushes?

SYLVIA, *angered:* To humiliate them, to make fools of them!

HARRIET: Oh!

SYLVIA: How can you be so . . . so . . . ? *Breaks off before she goes too far.* Harriet, please . . . leave me alone, will you?

HARRIET: This is not normal. Murray says the same thing. I swear to God, he came home last night and says, "She's got to stop thinking about those Germans." And you know how he loves current events. *Sylvia is staring ahead.* I'll see if the duck looks good, if not I'll get chops. Can I get you something now?

SYLVIA: No, I'm fine, thanks.

HARRIET, *moves upstage of Sylvia, turns:* I'm going.

SYLVIA: Yes.

> *She returns to her paper. Harriet watches anxiously for a moment, out of Sylvia's sight line, then exits. Sylvia turns a page, absorbed in the paper. Suddenly she turns in shock—Phillip is standing behind her. He holds a small paper bag.*

SYLVIA: Oh! I didn't hear you come in.

GELLBURG: I tiptoed, in case you were dozing off . . . *His dour smile.* I bought you some sour pickles.

SYLVIA: Oh, that's nice! Later, maybe. You have one.

GELLBURG: I'll wait. *Awkwardly but determined:* I was passing Greenberg's on Flatbush Avenue and I suddenly remembered how you used to love them. Remember?

SYLVIA: Thanks, that's nice of you. What were you doing on Flatbush Avenue?

GELLBURG: There's a property across from A&S. I'm probably going to foreclose.

SYLVIA: Oh that's sad. Are they nice people?

GELLBURG, *shrugs:* People are people—I gave them two extensions but they'll never manage . . . nothing up here. *Taps his temple.*

SYLVIA: Aren't you early?

GELLBURG: I got worried about you. Doctor come?

SYLVIA: He called; he has the results of the tests but he wants to come tomorrow when he has more time to talk to me. He's really very nice.

GELLBURG: How was it today?

SYLVIA: I'm so sorry about this.

GELLBURG: You'll get better, don't worry about it. Oh!— there's a letter from the captain. *Takes it out of his jacket.*

SYLVIA: Jerome?

GELLBURG, *terrific personal pride:* Read it.

She reads; his purse-mouthed grin is intense.

That's your son. General MacArthur talked to him twice.

SYLVIA: Fort Sill?

GELLBURG: Oklahoma. *He's going to lecture them on artillery!*
In *Fort Sill!* That's the field-artillery center.

She looks up dumbly.

That's like being invited to the Vatican to lecture the
Pope.

SYLVIA: Imagine. *She folds the letter and hands it back to him.*

GELLBURG, *restraining greater resentment:* I don't understand
this attitude.

SYLVIA: Why? I'm happy for him.

GELLBURG: You don't seem happy to me.

SYLVIA: I'll never get used to it. Who goes in the army?
Men who can't do anything else.

GELLBURG: I wanted people to see that a Jew doesn't have
to be a lawyer or a doctor or a businessman.

SYLVIA: That's fine, but why must it be Jerome?

GELLBURG: For a Jewish boy, West Point is an honor! Without Mr. Case's connections, he never would have gotten
in. He could be the first Jewish general in the United
States Army. Doesn't it mean something to be his mother?

SYLVIA, *with an edge of resentment:* Well, I said I'm glad.

GELLBURG: Don't be upset. *Looks about impatiently.* You
know, when you get on your feet I'll help you hang the
new drapes.

SYLVIA: I started to . . .

GELLBURG: But they've been here over a month.

SYLVIA: Well this happened, I'm sorry.

GELLBURG: You have to occupy yourself is all I'm saying,
Sylvia, you can't give in to this.

SYLVIA, *near an outburst:* Well I'm sorry—I'm sorry about
everything!

GELLBURG: Please, don't get upset, I take it back!

A moment; stalemate.

SYLVIA: I wonder what my tests show.

Gellburg is silent.

That the specialist did.

GELLBURG: I went to see Doctor Hyman last night.

SYLVIA: You did? Why didn't you mention it?

GELLBURG: I wanted to think over what he said.

SYLVIA: What did he say?

> *With a certain deliberateness, Gellburg goes over to
> her and gives her a kiss on the cheek.*

SYLVIA, *she is embarrassed and vaguely alarmed:* Phillip! *A little
uncomprehending laugh.*

GELLBURG: I want to change some things. About the way
I've been doing.

> *He stands there for a moment perfectly still, then rolls
> her chair closer to the bed on which he now sits and
> takes her hand. She doesn't quite know what to
> make of this, but doesn't remove her hand.*

SYLVIA: Well what did he say?

GELLBURG, *he pats her hand:* I'll tell you in a minute. I'm
thinking about a Dodge.

SYLVIA: A Dodge?

GELLBURG: I want to teach you to drive. So you can go where you like, visit your mother in the afternoon. —I want you to be happy, Sylvia.

SYLVIA, *surprised:* Oh.

GELLBURG: We have the money, we could do a lot of things. Maybe see Washington, D.C. . . . It's supposed to be a very strong car, you know.

SYLVIA: But aren't they all black?—Dodges?

GELLBURG: Not all. I've seen a couple of green ones.

SYLVIA: You like green?

GELLBURG: It's only a color. You'll get used to it. —Or Chicago. It's really a big city, you know.

SYLVIA: Tell me what Doctor Hyman said.

GELLBURG, *gets himself set:* He thinks it could all be coming from your mind. Like a . . . a fear of some kind got into you. Psychological.

She is still, listening.

Are you afraid of something?

SYLVIA, *a slow shrug, a shake of her head:* . . . I don't know, I don't think so. What kind of fear, what does he mean?

GELLBURG: Well, he explains it better, but . . . like in a war, people get so afraid they go blind temporarily. What they call shell-shock. But once they feel safer it goes away.

SYLVIA: What about the tests the Mount Sinai man did?

GELLBURG: They can't find anything wrong with your body.

SYLVIA: But I'm numb!

GELLBURG: He claims being very frightened could be doing it. —Are you?

SYLVIA: I don't know.

GELLBURG: Personally. . . . Can I tell you what I think?

SYLVIA: What.

GELLBURG: I think it's this whole Nazi business.

SYLVIA: But it's in the paper—they're smashing up the Jewish stores . . . Should I not read the paper? The streets are covered with broken glass!

GELLBURG: Yes, but you don't have to be constantly . . .

SYLVIA: It's ridiculous. I can't move my legs from reading a newspaper?

GELLBURG: He didn't say that; but I'm wondering if you're too involved with . . .

SYLVIA: It's ridiculous.

GELLBURG: Well you talk to him tomorrow. *Pause. He comes back to her and takes her hand, his need open.* You've got to get better, Sylvia.

SYLVIA, *she sees his tortured face and tries to laugh:* What is this, am I dying or something?

GELLBURG: How can you say that?

SYLVIA: I've never seen such a look in your face.

GELLBURG: Oh no-no-no . . . I'm just worried.

SYLVIA: I don't understand what's happening . . . *She turns away on the verge of tears.*

GELLBURG: . . . I never realized . . . *Sudden sharpness* . . . look at me, will you?

> *She turns to him; he glances down at the floor.*

I wouldn't know what to do without you, Sylvia, honest to God. I . . . *Immense difficulty.* I love you.

SYLVIA, *a dead, bewildered laugh:* What is this?

GELLBURG: You have to get better. If I'm ever doing something wrong I'll change it. Let's try to be different. All right? And you too, you've got to do what the doctors tell you.

SYLVIA: What can I do? Here I sit and they say there's nothing wrong with me.

GELLBURG: Listen . . . I think Hyman is a very smart man . . . *He lifts her hand and kisses her knuckle; embarrassed and smiling.* When we were talking, something came to mind; that maybe if we could sit down with him, the three of us, and maybe talk about . . . you know . . . everything.

Pause.

SYLVIA: That doesn't matter anymore, Phillip.

GELLBURG, *an embarrassed grin:* How do you know? Maybe . . .

SYLVIA: It's too late for that.

GELLBURG, *once launched he is terrified:* Why? Why is it too late?

SYLVIA: I'm surprised you're still worried about it.

GELLBURG: I'm not worried, I just think about it now and then.

SYLVIA: Well it's too late, dear, it doesn't matter anymore. *She draws back her hand.*

Pause.

GELLBURG: . . . Well all right. But if you wanted to I'd . . .

SYLVIA: We did talk about it, I took you to Rabbi Steiner about it twice, what good did it do?

GELLBURG: In those days I still thought it would change by itself. I was so young, I didn't understand such things. It came out of nowhere and I thought it would go the same way.

SYLVIA: I'm sorry, Phillip, it didn't come out of nowhere.

Silent, he evades her eyes.

SYLVIA: You regretted you got married.

GELLBURG: I didn't "regret" it . . .

SYLVIA: You did, dear. You don't have to be ashamed of it.

A long silence.

GELLBURG: I'm going to tell you the truth—in those days I thought that if we separated I wouldn't die of it. I admit that.

SYLVIA: I always knew that.

GELLBURG: But I haven't felt that way in years now.

SYLVIA: Well I'm here. *Spreads her arms out, a wildly ironical look in her eyes.* Here I am, Phillip!

GELLBURG, *offended:* The way you say that is not very . . .

SYLVIA: Not very what? I'm here; I've been here a long time.

GELLBURG, *a helpless surge of anger:* I'm trying to tell you something!

SYLVIA, *openly taunting him now:* But I said I'm here!

> *Gellburg moves about as she speaks, as though trying to find an escape or a way in.*

I'm here for my mother's sake, and Jerome's sake, and everybody's sake except mine, but I'm here and here I am. And now finally you want to talk about it, now when I'm turning into an old woman? How do you want me to say it? Tell me, dear, I'll say it the way you want me to. What should I say?

GELLBURG, *insulted and guilty:* I want you to stand up.

SYLVIA: I can't stand up.

> *He takes both her hands.*

GELLBURG: You can. Now come on. Stand up.

SYLVIA: I can't!

GELLBURG: You can stand up, Sylvia. Now lean to me and get on your feet.

He pulls her up; then steps aside, releasing her; she collapses on the floor. He stands over her.

What are you trying to do? *He goes to his knees to yell into her face: What are you trying to do, Sylvia!*

She looks at him in terror at the mystery before her.

Blackout.

The Lone Cellist plays. Then lights go down . . .

Dr. Hyman's office. He is in riding boots and a sweater. Harriet is seated beside his desk.

HARRIET: My poor sister. And they have everything! But how can it be in the mind if she's so paralyzed?

HYMAN: Her numbness is random, it doesn't follow the nerve paths; only part of the thighs are affected, part of the calves, it makes no physiological sense. I have a few things I'd like to ask you, all right?

HARRIET: You know, I'm glad it's you taking care of her, my husband says the same thing.

HYMAN: Thank you . . .

HARRIET: You probably don't remember, but you once took out our cousin Roslyn Fein? She said you were great.

HYMAN: Roslyn Fein. When?

HARRIET: She's very tall and reddish-blond hair? She had a real crush . . .

HYMAN, *pleased:* When was this?

HARRIET: Oh—NYU, maybe twenty-five years ago. She adored you; seriously, she said you were really *great.* *Laughs knowingly.* Used to take her to Coney Island swimming, and so on.

HYMAN, *laughs with her:* Oh. Well give her my regards.

HARRIET: I hardly see her, she lives in Florida.

HYMAN, *pressing on:* I'd like you to tell me about Sylvia; — before she collapsed, was there any sign of some shock, or anything? Something threatening her?

HARRIET, *thinks for a moment, shrugs, shaking her head:* Listen, I'll tell you something funny—to me sometimes she seems . . . I was going to say happy, but it's more like . . . I don't know . . . like this is how she wants to be. I mean since the collapse. Don't you think so?

HYMAN: Well I never really knew her before. What about this fascination with the Nazis—she ever talk to you about that?

HARRIET: Only this last couple of weeks. I don't understand it, they're in *Germany,* how can she be so frightened, it's across the ocean, isn't it?

HYMAN: Yes. But in a way it isn't. *He stares, shaking his head, lost.* . . . She's very sensitive; she really sees the people in those photographs. They're alive to her.

HARRIET, *suddenly near tears:* My poor sister!

HYMAN: Tell me about Phillip.

HARRIET: Phillip? *Shrugs.* Phillip is Phillip.

HYMAN: You like him?

HARRIET: Well he's my brother-in-law . . . You mean personally.

HYMAN: Yes.

HARRIET, *takes a breath to lie:* . . . He can be very sweet, you know. But suddenly he'll turn around and talk to you like you've got four legs and long ears. The men—not that they don't respect him—but they'd just as soon not play cards with him if they can help it.

HYMAN: Really. Why?

HARRIET: Well, God forbid you have an opinion—you open your mouth and he gives you that Republican look down his nose and your brains dry up. Not that I don't *like* him . . .

HYMAN: How did he and Sylvia meet?

HARRIET: She was head bookkeeper at Empire Steel over there in Long Island City . . .

HYMAN: She must have been very young.

HARRIET: . . . Twenty; just out of high school practically and she's head bookkeeper. According to my husband, God gave Sylvia all the brains and the rest of us the big feet! The reason they met was the company took out a mortgage and she had to explain all the accounts to Phillip—he used to say, "I fell in love with her figures!" *Hyman laughs.* Why should I lie?—personally to me, he's a little bit a prune. Like he never stops with the whole Jewish part of it.

HYMAN: He doesn't like being Jewish.

HARRIET: Well yes and no—like Jerome being the only Jewish captain, he's proud of that. And him being the only one ever worked for Brooklyn Guarantee—he's proud of that too, but at the same time . . .

HYMAN: . . . He'd rather not be one.

HARRIET: . . . Look, he's a mystery to me. I don't understand him and I never will.

HYMAN: What about the marriage? I promise you this is strictly between us.

HARRIET: What can I tell you, the marriage is a marriage.

HYMAN: And?

HARRIET: I shouldn't talk about it.

HYMAN: It stays in this office. Tell me. They ever break up?

HARRIET: Oh God no! Why should they? He's a wonderful
provider. There's no Depression for Phillip, you know.
And it would kill our mother, she worships Phillip, she'd
never outlive it. No-no, it's out of the question, Sylvia's
not that kind of woman, although . . . *Breaks off.*

HYMAN: Come, Harriet, I need to know these things!

HARRIET: . . . Well I guess everybody knows it, so . . .
Takes a breath. I think they came very close to it one time
. . . when he hit her with the steak.

HYMAN: Hit her with a *steak?*

SYLVIA: It was overdone.

HYMAN: What do you mean, hit her?

SYLVIA: He picked it up off the plate and slapped her in the
face with it.

HYMAN: And then what?

HARRIET: Well if my mother hadn't patched it up I don't
know what would have happened and then he went out

and bought her that gorgeous beaver coat, and repainted
the whole house, and he's tight as a drum, you know, so
it was hard for him. I don't know what to tell you. —
Why?—you think *he* could have frightened her like this?

HYMAN, *hesitates:* I don't know yet. The whole thing is very
strange.

> *Something darkens Harriet's expression and she be-
> gins to shake her head from side to side and she bursts
> into tears. He comes and puts an arm around her.*

HYMAN: What is it?

HARRIET: All her life she did nothing but love everybody!

HYMAN, *reaches out to take her hand:* Harriet.

> *She looks at him.*

What do you want to tell me?

HARRIET: I don't know if it's right to talk about. But of
course, it's years and years ago . . .

HYMAN: None of this will ever be repeated; believe me.

HARRIET: Well . . . every first of the year when Uncle
Myron was still alive we'd all go down to his basement
for a New Year's party. I'm talking like fifteen, sixteen
years ago. He's dead now, Myron, but . . . he was . . .

you know . . . *Small laugh* . . . a little comical; he always
kept this shoebox full of . . . you know, these postcards.

HYMAN: You mean . . .

HARRIET: Yes. French. You know, naked women, and men
with these great big . . . you know . . . they hung down
like salamis. And everybody'd pass them around and die
laughing. It was exactly the same thing every New Year's.
But this time, all of a sudden, Phillip . . . we thought he'd
lost his mind . . .

HYMAN: What happened?

HARRIET: Well Sylvia's in the middle of laughing and he
grabs the postcard out of her hand and he turns around
screaming—I mean, really screaming—that we're all a
bunch of morons and idiots and God knows what, and
throws her up the stairs. Bang! It cracked the bannister, I
can still hear it. *Catches her breath.* I tell you it was months
before anybody'd talk to him again. Because everybody
on the block loves Sylvia.

HYMAN: What do you suppose made him do that?

HARRIET, *shrugs:* . . . Well if you listen to some of the
men—but of course some of the dirty minds on this block
. . . if you spread it over the backyard you'd get tomatoes
six feet high.

HYMAN: Why?—what'd they say?

HARRIET: Well that the reason he got so mad was because he couldn't . . . you know . . .

HYMAN: Oh really.

HARRIET: . . . anymore.

HYMAN: But they made up.

HARRIET: Listen, to be truthful you have to say it—although it'll sound crazy . . .

HYMAN: What.

HARRIET: You watch him sometimes when they've got people over and she's talking—he'll sit quietly in the corner, and the expression on that man's face when he's watching her—it could almost break your heart.

HYMAN: Why?

HARRIET: He adores her!

Blackout.

SCENE FOUR

The cellist plays, and is gone.

Stanton Case is getting ready to leave his office. Putting on his blazer and a captain's cap and a foulard. He has a great natural authority, an almost childishly naive self-assurance. Gellburg enters.

CASE: Good!—you're back. I was just leaving.

GELLBURG: I'm sorry. I got caught in traffic over in Crown Heights.

CASE: I wanted to talk to you again about 611. Sit down for a moment.

Both sit.

We're sailing out through the Narrows in about an hour.

GELLBURG: Beautiful day for it.

CASE: Are you all right? You don't look well.

GELLBURG: Oh no, I'm fine.

CASE: Good. Have you come to anything final on 611? I like the price, I can tell you that right off.

GELLBURG: Yes, the price is not bad, but I'm still . . .

CASE: I've walked past it again; I think with some renovation it would make a fine annex for the Harvard Club.

GELLBURG: It's a very nice structure, yes. I'm not final on it yet but I have a few comments . . . unless you've got to get on the water right away.

CASE: I have a few minutes. Go ahead.

GELLBURG: . . . Before I forget—we got a very nice letter from Jerome.

No reaction from Case.

My boy.

CASE: Oh yes!—how is he doing?

GELLBURG: They're bringing him out to Fort Sill . . . some kind of lecture on artillery.

CASE: Really, now! Well, isn't that nice! . . . Then he's really intending to make a career in the army.

GELLBURG, *surprised Case isn't aware:* Oh absolutely.

CASE: Well that's good, isn't it. It's quite surprising for one of you people—for some reason I'd assumed he just wanted the education.

GELLBURG: Oh no. It's his life. I'll never know how to thank you.

CASE: No trouble at all. The Point can probably use a few of you people to keep the rest of them awake. Now what's this about 611?

GELLBURG, *sets himself in all dignity:* You might recall, we used the ABC Plumbing Contractors on a couple of buildings?

CASE: ABC? —I don't recall. What have they got to do with it?

GELLBURG: They're located in the neighborhood, just off Broadway, and on a long shot I went over to see Mr. Liebfreund—he runs ABC. I was wondering if they may have done any work for Wanamaker's.

CASE: Wanamaker's! What's Wanamaker's got to do with it?

GELLBURG: I buy my shirts in Wanamaker's, and last time I was in there I caught my shoe on a splinter sticking up out of the floor.

CASE: Well that store is probably fifty years old.

GELLBURG: Closer to seventy-five. I tripped and almost fell down; this was very remarkable to me, that they would leave a floor in such condition. So I began wondering about it . . .

CASE: About what?

GELLBURG: Number 611 is two blocks from Wanamaker's. *A little extra-wise grin.* They're the biggest business in the area, a whole square block, after all. Anyway, sure enough, turns out ABC does all Wanamaker's plumbing work. And Liebfreund tells me he's had to keep patching up their boilers *because they canceled installation of new boilers last winter.* A permanent cancellation.

Pause.

CASE: And what do you make of that?

GELLBURG: I think it could mean they're either moving the store, or maybe going out of business.

CASE: *Wanamaker's?*

GELLBURG: It's possible, I understand the family is practically died out. Either way, if Wanamaker's disappears, Mr. Case, that neighborhood in my opinion is no longer prime. Also, I called Kevin Sullivan over at Title Guarantee and he says they turned down 611 last year and he can't remember why.

CASE: Then what are you telling me?

GELLBURG: I would not touch Number 611 with a ten-foot pole—unless you can get it at a good defensive price. If that neighborhood starts to slide, 611 is a great big slice of lemon.

CASE: Well. That's very disappointing. It would have made a wonderful club annex.

GELLBURG: With a thing like the Harvard Club you have got to think of the far distant future, Mr. Case, I don't have to tell you that, and the future of that part of Broadway is a definite possible negative. *Raising a monitory finger:* I emphasize "possible," mind you; only God can predict.

CASE: Well I must say, I would never have thought of Wanamaker's disappearing. You've been more than thorough, Gellburg, we appreciate it. I've got to run now, but we'll talk about this further . . . *Glances at his watch.* Mustn't miss the tide . . . *Moves, indicates.* Take a brandy if you like. Wife all right?

GELLBURG: Oh yes, she's fine!

CASE, *the faint shadow of a warning:* Sure everything's all right with you—we don't want you getting sick now.

GELLBURG: Oh no, I'm very well, very well.

CASE: I'll be back on Monday, we'll go into this further. *Indicates.* Take a brandy if you like.

Case exits rather jauntily.

GELLBURG: Yes, sir, I might!

Gellburg stands alone; with a look of self-satisfaction starts to raise the glass.

Blackout.

The cello plays, and the music falls away.

Sylvia in bed, reading a book. She looks up as Hyman enters. He is in his riding clothes. Sylvia has a certain excitement at seeing him.

SYLVIA: Oh, doctor!

HYMAN: I let myself in, hope I didn't scare you . . .

SYLVIA: Oh no, I'm glad. Sit down. You been riding?

HYMAN: Yes. All the way down to Brighton Beach, nice long ride—I expected to see you jumping rope by now.

Sylvia laughs, embarrassed.

I think you're just trying to get out of doing the dishes.

SYLVIA, *strained laugh:* Oh stop. You really love riding, don't you?

HYMAN: Well there's no telephone on a horse.

She laughs.

Ocean Parkway is like a German forest this time of the morning—riding under that archway of maple trees is like poetry.

SYLVIA: Wonderful. I never did anything like that.

HYMAN: Well, let's go—I'll take you out and teach you sometime. Have you been trying the exercise?

SYLVIA: I can't do it.

HYMAN, *shaking a finger at her:* You've *got* to do it, Sylvia. You could end up permanently crippled. Let's have a look.

> *He sits on the bed and draws the cover off her legs, then raises her nightgown. She inhales with a certain anticipation as he does so. He feels her toes.*

You feel this at all?

SYLVIA: Well . . . not really.

HYMAN: I'm going to pinch your toe. Ready?

SYLVIA: All right.

> *He pinches her big toe sharply; she doesn't react. He rests a palm on her leg.*

HYMAN: Your skin feels a little too cool. You're going to lose your muscle tone if you don't move. Your legs will begin to lose volume and shrink . . .

SYLVIA, *tears threaten:* I know . . . !

HYMAN: And look what beautiful legs you have, Sylvia. I'm afraid you're getting comfortable in this condition . . .

SYLVIA: I'm not. I keep trying to move them . . .

HYMAN: But look now—here it's eleven in the morning and you're happily tucked into bed like it's midnight.

SYLVIA: But I've tried . . . ! Are you really sure it's not a virus of some kind?

HYMAN: There's nothing. Sylvia, you have a strong beautiful body . . .

SYLVIA: But what can I do, I can't feel anything!

> *She sits up with her face raised to him; he stands and moves abruptly away. Then turning back to her . . .*

HYMAN: I really should find someone else for you.

SYLVIA: Why!—I don't want anyone else!

HYMAN: You're a very attractive woman, don't you know that?

Deeply excited, Sylvia glances away shyly.

HYMAN: Sylvia, listen to me . . . I haven't been this moved by a woman in a very long time.

SYLVIA: . . . Well, you mustn't get anyone else.

Pause.

HYMAN: Tell me the truth, Sylvia. Sylvia? How did this happen to you?

SYLVIA, *she avoids his gaze:* I don't know. *Sylvia's anxiety rises as he speaks now.*

HYMAN: . . . I'm going to be straight with you; I thought this was going to be simpler than it's turning out to be, and I care about you too much to play a game with your health. I can't deny my vanity. I have a lot of it, but I have to face it—I know you want to tell me something and I don't know how to get it out of you. *Sylvia covers her face, ashamed.* You're a responsible woman, Sylvia, you have to start helping me, you can't just lie there and expect a miracle to lift you to your feet. You tell me now —what should I know?

SYLVIA: I would tell you if I knew! *Hyman turns away defeated and impatient.* Couldn't we just talk and maybe I could

. . . *Breaks off.* I like you. A lot. I love when you talk to me . . . couldn't we just . . . like for a few minutes. . . .

HYMAN: Okay. What do you want to talk about?

SYLVIA: Please. Be patient. I'm . . . I'm trying. *Relieved; a fresher mood:* —Harriet says you used to take out our cousin Roslyn Fein.

HYMAN, *smiles, shrugs:* It's possible, I don't remember.

SYLVIA: Well you had so many, didn't you.

HYMAN: When I was younger.

SYLVIA: Roslyn said you used to do acrobatics on the beach? And all the girls would stand around going crazy for you.

HYMAN: That's a long time ago. . . .

SYLVIA: And you'd take them under the boardwalk. *Laughs.*

HYMAN: Nobody had money for anything else. Didn't you used to go to the beach?

SYLVIA: Sure. But I never did anything like that.

HYMAN: You must have been very shy.

SYLVIA: I guess. But I had to look out for my sisters, being the eldest . . .

HYMAN: Can we talk about Phillip?

Caught unaware, her eyes show fear.

I'd really like to, unless you . . .

SYLVIA, *challenged:* No!—It's all right.

HYMAN: . . . Are you afraid right now?

SYLVIA: No, not . . . Yes.

Picks up the book beside her.

Have you read *Anthony Adverse?*

HYMAN: No, but I hear it's sold a million copies.

SYLVIA: It's wonderful. I rent it from Womraths.

HYMAN: Was Phillip your first boyfriend?

SYLVIA: The first serious.

HYMAN: He's a fine man.

SYLVIA: Yes, he is.

HYMAN: Is he interesting to be with?

SYLVIA: Interesting?

HYMAN: Do you have things to talk about?

SYLVIA: Well . . . business, mostly. I was head bookkeeper for Empire Steel in Long Island City . . . years ago, when we met, I mean.

HYMAN: He didn't want you to work?

SYLVIA: No.

HYMAN: I imagine you were a good businesswoman.

SYLVIA: Oh, I loved it! I've always enjoyed . . . you know, people depending on me.

HYMAN: Yes. —Do I frighten you, talking like this?

SYLVIA: A little. —But I want you to.

HYMAN: Why?

SYLVIA: I don't know. You make me feel . . . hopeful.

HYMAN: You mean of getting better?

SYLVIA: —Of myself. Of getting . . . *Breaks off.*

HYMAN: Getting what?

> *She shakes her head, refusing to go on.*

. . . Free?

> *She suddenly kisses the palm of his hand. He wipes*
> *her hair away from her eyes. He stands up and walks*
> *a few steps away.*

HYMAN: I want you to raise your knees.

> *She doesn't move.*

Come, bring up your knees.

SYLVIA, *she tries:* I can't!

HYMAN: You can. I want you to send your thoughts into
your hips. Tense your hips. Think of the bones in your
hips. Come on now. The strongest muscles in your body
are right there, you still have tremendous power there.
Tense your hips.

> *She is tensing.*

Now tense your thighs. Those are long dense muscles
with tremendous power. Do it, draw up your knees.
Come on, raise your knees. Keep it up. Concentrate.
Raise it. Do it for me.

> *With an exhaled gasp she gives up. Remaining yards*
> *away . . .*

Your body strength must be marvelous. The depth of your flesh must be wonderful. Why are you cut off from yourself? You should be dancing, you should be stretching out in the sun. . . . Sylvia, I know you know more than you're saying, why can't you open up to me? Speak to me. Sylvia? Say anything.

She looks at him in silence.

I promise I won't tell a soul. What is in your mind right now?

A pause.

SYLVIA: Tell me about Germany.

HYMAN, *surprised:* Germany. Why Germany?

SYLVIA: Why did you go there to study?

HYMAN: The American medical schools have quotas on Jews, I would have had to wait for years and maybe never get in.

SYLVIA: But they hate Jews there, don't they?

HYMAN: These Nazis can't possibly last— Why are you so preoccupied with them?

SYLVIA: I don't know. But when I saw that picture in the *Times*—with those two old men on their knees in the street . . . *Presses her ears.* I swear, I almost heard that crowd laughing, and ridiculing them. But nobody really wants to talk about it. I mean Phillip never even wants to talk about being Jewish, except—you know—to joke about it the way people do . . .

HYMAN: What would you like to say to Phillip about it?

SYLVIA, *with an empty laugh, a head shake:* I don't even know! Just to talk about it . . . it's almost like there's something in me that . . . it's silly . . .

HYMAN: No, it's interesting. What do you mean, something in you?

SYLVIA: I have no word for it, I don't know what I'm saying, it's like . . . *She presses her chest.*—something alive, like a child almost, except it's a very dark thing . . . and it frightens me!

> *Hyman moves his hand to calm her and she grabs it.*

HYMAN: That was hard to say, wasn't it. *Sylvia nods.* You have a lot of courage.—We'll talk more, but I want you to try something now. I'll stand here, and I want you to imagine something. *Sylvia turns to him, curious.* I want you to imagine that we've made love.

> *Startled, she laughs tensely. He joins this laugh as though it is a game.*

I've made love to you. And now it's over and we are
lying together. And you begin to tell me some secret
things. Things that are way down deep in your heart.
Slight pause. Sylvia—

> *Hyman comes around the bed, bends, and kisses her
> on the cheek.*

Tell me about Phillip.
*Sylvia is silent, does not grasp his head to hold him. He straight-
ens up.* Think about it. We'll talk tomorrow again. Okay?

> *Hyman exits. Sylvia lies there inert for a moment.
> Then she tenses with effort, trying to raise her knee.
> It doesn't work. She reaches down and lifts the knee,
> and then the other and lies there that way. Then she
> lets her knees spread apart . . .*

> *Blackout.*

SCENE SIX

The cellist plays, then is gone.

Hyman's office. Gellburg is seated. Immediately Margaret enters with a cup of cocoa and a file folder. She hands the cup to Gellburg.

GELLBURG: Cocoa?

MARGARET: I drink a lot of it, it calms the nerves. Have you lost weight?

GELLBURG, *impatience with her prying:* A little, I think.

MARGARET: Did you always sigh so much?

GELLBURG: Sigh?

MARGARET: You probably don't realize you're doing it. You should have him listen to your heart.

GELLBURG: No-no, I think I'm all right. *Sighs.* I guess I've always sighed. Is that a sign of something?

MARGARET: Not necessarily; but ask Harry. He's just finishing with a patient. —There's no change, I understand.

GELLBURG: No, she's the same. *Impatiently hands her the cup.* I can't drink this.

MARGARET: Are you eating at all?

GELLBURG, *suddenly shifting his mode:* I came to talk to *him.*

MARGARET, *sharply:* I was only trying to be helpful!

GELLBURG: I'm kind of upset, I didn't mean any . . .

Hyman enters, surprising her. She exits, insulted.

HYMAN: I'm sorry. But she means well.

Gellburg silently nods, irritation intact.

HYMAN: It won't happen again. *He takes his seat.* I have to admit, though, she has a very good diagnostic sense. Women are more instinctive sometimes . . .

GELLBURG: Excuse me, I don't come here to be talking to her.

HYMAN, *a kidding laugh:* Oh, come on, Phillip, take it easy. What's Sylvia doing?

GELLBURG, *it takes him a moment to compose himself:* . . . I don't know what she's doing.

> *Hyman waits. Gellburg has a tortured look; now he seems to brace himself, and faces the doctor with what seems a haughty air.*

I decided to try to do what you advised. —About the loving.

HYMAN: . . . Yes?

GELLBURG: So I decided to try to do it with her.

HYMAN: . . . Sex?

GELLBURG: What then, handball? Of course sex.

> *The openness of this hostility mystifies Hyman, who becomes conciliatory.*

HYMAN: . . . Well, do you mean you've done it or you're going to?

GELLBURG, *long pause; he seems not to be sure he wants to continue. Now he sounds reasonable again:* You see, we haven't been really . . . together. For . . quite a long time. *Correcting:* I mean specially since this started to happen.

HYMAN: You mean the last two weeks.

GELLBURG: Well yes. *Great discomfort.* And some time before that.

HYMAN: I see. *But he desists from asking how long a time before that. A pause.*

GELLBURG: So I thought maybe it would help her if . . . you know.

HYMAN: Yes, I think the warmth would help. In fact, to be candid, Phillip—I'm beginning to wonder if this whole fear of the Nazis isn't because she feels . . . extremely vulnerable; I'm in no sense trying to blame you but . . . a woman who doesn't feel loved can get very disoriented you know? —lost. *He has noticed a strangeness.*—Something wrong?

GELLBURG: She says she's not being loved?

HYMAN: No–no. I'm talking about how she may feel.

GELLBURG: Listen . . . *Struggles for a moment; now firmly.* I'm wondering if you could put me in touch with somebody.

HYMAN: You mean for yourself?

GELLBURG: I don't know; I'm not sure what they do, though.

HYMAN: I know a very good man at the hospital, if you want me to set it up.

GELLBURG: Well maybe not yet, let me let you know.

HYMAN: Sure.

GELLBURG: Your wife says I sigh a lot. Does that mean something?

HYMAN: Could just be tension. Come in when you have a little time, I'll look you over. . . . Am I wrong?—you sound like something's happened . . .

GELLBURG: This whole thing is against me . . . *Attempting a knowing grin.* But you know that.

HYMAN: Now wait a minute . . .

GELLBURG: She knows what she's doing, you're not blind.

HYMAN: What happened, why are you saying this?

GELLBURG: I was late last night—I had to be in Jersey all afternoon, a problem we have there—she was sound asleep. So I made myself some spaghetti. Usually she puts something out for me.

HYMAN: She has no problem cooking.

GELLBURG: I told you—she gets around the kitchen fine in the wheelchair. Flora shops in the morning—that's the maid. Although I'm beginning to wonder if Sylvia gets out and walks around when I leave the house.

HYMAN: It's impossible.—She is paralyzed, Phillip, it's not a trick—she's suffering.

GELLBURG, *a sideways glance at Hyman:* What do you discuss with her?—You know, she talks like you see right through her.

HYMAN, *a laugh:* I wish I could! We talk about getting her to walk, that's all. This thing is not against you, Phillip, believe me. *Slight laugh.*—I wish you could trust me, kid!

GELLBURG, *seems momentarily on the edge of being reassured and studies Hyman's face for a moment, nodding very slightly:* I would never believe I could talk this way to another person. I do trust you.

Pause.

HYMAN: Good!—I'm listening, go ahead.

GELLBURG: The first time we talked you asked me if we . . . how many times a week.

HYMAN: Yes.

GELLBURG, *nods:* . . . I have a problem sometimes.

HYMAN: Oh.—Well that's fairly common, you know.

GELLBURG, *relieved:* You see it often?

HYMAN: Oh very often, yes.

GELLBURG, *a tense challenging smile:* Ever happen to you?

HYMAN, *surprised:* . . . Me? Well sure, a few times. Is this something recent?

GELLBURG: Well . . . yes. Recent and also . . . *breaks off, indicating the past with a gesture of his hand.*

HYMAN: I see. It doesn't help if you're under tension, you know.

GELLBURG: Yes, I was wondering that.

HYMAN: Just don't start thinking it's the end of the world because it's not—you're still a young man. Think of it like the ocean—it goes out but it always comes in again. But the thing to keep in mind is that she loves you and wants you.

Gellburg looks wide-eyed.

You know that, don't you?

GELLBURG, *silently nods for an instant:* My sister-in-law Harriet says you were a real hotshot on the beach years ago.

HYMAN: Years ago, yes.

GELLBURG: I used to wonder if it's because Sylvia's the only
one I was ever with.

HYMAN: Why would that matter?

GELLBURG: I don't know exactly—it used to prey on my
mind that . . . maybe she expected more.

HYMAN: Yes. Well that's a common idea, you know. In fact,
some men take on a lot of women not out of confidence
but because they're afraid to lose it.

GELLBURG, *fascinated:* Huh! I'd never of thought of that.
—A doctor must get a lot of peculiar cases, I bet.

HYMAN, *with utter intimacy:* Everybody's peculiar in one way
or another but I'm not here to judge people. Why don't
you try to tell me what happened? *His grin; making light
of it.* Come on, give it a shot.

GELLBURG: All right . . . *Sighs.* I get into bed. She's sound
asleep . . . *Breaks off. Resumes; something transcendent seems
to enter him.* Nothing like it ever happened to me, I got
a . . . a big yen for her. She's even more beautiful when
she sleeps. I gave her a kiss. On the mouth. She didn't
wake up. I never had such a yen in my life.

Long pause.

HYMAN: And?

Gellburg silent.

Did you make love?

GELLBURG, *an incongruous look of terror, he becomes rigid as though about to decide whether to dive into icy water or flee:* . . . Yes.

HYMAN, *a quickening, something tentative in Gellburg mystifies:* How did she react? —It's been some time since you did it, you say.

GELLBURG: Well yes.

HYMAN: Then what was the reaction?

GELLBURG: She was . . . *Searches for the word.* Gasping. It was really something. I thought of what you told me—about loving her now; I felt I'd brought her out of it. I was almost sure of it. She was like a different woman than I ever knew.

HYMAN: That's wonderful. Did she move her legs?

GELLBURG, *unprepared for that question:* . . . I think so.

HYMAN: Well did she or didn't she?

GELLBURG: Well I was so excited I didn't really notice, but I guess she must have.

HYMAN: That's wonderful, why are you so upset?

GELLBURG: Well let me finish, there's more to it.

HYMAN: Sorry, go ahead.

GELLBURG: —I brought her some breakfast this morning and—you know—started to—you know—talk a little about it. She looked at me like I was crazy. She claims she doesn't remember doing it. It never happened.

> *Hyman is silent, plays with a pen. Something evasive in this.*

How could she not remember it?

HYMAN: You're sure she was awake?

GELLBURG: How could she not be?

HYMAN: Did she say anything during the . . . ?

GELLBURG: Well no, but she's never said much.

HYMAN: Did she open her eyes?

GELLBURG: I'm not sure. We were in the dark, but she usually keeps them closed. *Impatiently:* But she was . . . she was groaning, panting . . . she had to be awake! And now to say she doesn't remember?

Shaken, Hyman gets up and moves; a pause.

HYMAN: So what do you think is behind it?

GELLBURG: Well what would any man think? She's trying to turn me into nothing!

HYMAN: Now wait, you're jumping to conclusions.

GELLBURG: Is such a thing possible? I want your medical opinion—could a woman not remember?

HYMAN, *a moment, then:* . . . How did she look when she said that; did she seem sincere about not remembering?

GELLBURG: She looked like I was talking about something on the moon. Finally, she said a terrible thing. I still can't get over it.

HYMAN: What'd she say?

GELLBURG: That I'd imagined doing it.

Long pause. Hyman doesn't move.

What's your opinion? Well . . . could a man imagine such a thing? Is that possible?

HYMAN, *after a moment:* Tell you what; supposing I have another talk with her and see what I can figure out?

GELLBURG, *angrily demanding:* You have an opinion, don't you?—How could a man imagine such a thing!

HYMAN: I don't know what to say . . .

GELLBURG: What do you mean you don't know what to say! It's impossible, isn't it? To invent such a thing?

HYMAN, *fear of being out of his depth:* Phillip, don't cross-examine me, I'm doing everythig I know to help you! —Frankly, I can't follow what you're telling me—you're sure in your own mind you had relations with her?

GELLBURG: How can you even ask me such a thing? Would I say it unless I was sure? *Stands shaking with fear and anger.* I don't understand your attitude! *He starts out.*

HYMAN: Phillip, please! *In fear he intercepts Gellburg.* What attitude, what are you talking about?

GELLBURG: I'm going to vomit, I swear—I don't feel well . . .

HYMAN: What happened . . . has she said something about me?

GELLBURG: About you? What do you mean? What could she say?

HYMAN: I don't understand why you're so upset with me!

GELLBURG: What are you doing!

HYMAN, *guiltily:* What am *I* doing! What are you talking about!

GELLBURG: She is trying to destroy me! And you stand there! And what do you do! Are you a doctor or what! *He goes right up to Hyman's face.* Why don't you give me a straight answer about anything! Everything is in-and-out and around-the-block! —Listen, I've made up my mind; I don't want you seeing her anymore.

HYMAN: I think she's the one has to decide that.

GELLBURG: I am deciding it! It's decided!

> *He storms out. Hyman stands there, guilty, alarmed.*
> *Margaret enters.*

MARGARET: Now what? *Seeing his anxiety:* Why are you looking like that?

> *He evasively returns to his desk chair.*

Are *you* in trouble?

HYMAN: Me! Cut it out, will you?

MARGARET: Cut what out? I asked a question—are you?

HYMAN: I said to cut it out, Margaret!

MARGARET: You don't realize how transparent you are. You're a pane of glass, Harry.

HYMAN, *laughs:* Nothing's happened. *Nothing has happened!* Why are you going on about it!

MARGARET: I will never understand it. Except I do, I guess; you believe women. Woman tells you the earth is flat and for that five minutes you're swept away, helpless.

HYMAN: You know what baffles me?

MARGARET: . . . And it's irritating.—What is it—just new ass all the time?

HYMAN: There's been nobody for at least ten or twelve years . . . more! I can't remember anymore! You know that!

MARGARET: What baffles you?

HYMAN: Why I take your suspicions seriously.

MARGARET: Oh that's easy. —You love the truth, Harry.

HYMAN, *a deep sigh, facing upward:* I'm exhausted.

MARGARET: What about asking Charley Whitman to see her?

HYMAN: She's frightened to death of psychiatry, she thinks it means she's crazy.

MARGARET: Well, she is, in a way, isn't she?

HYMAN: I don't see it that way at all.

MARGARET: Getting this hysterical about something on the other side of the world is sane?

HYMAN: When she talks about it, it's not the other side of the world it's on the next block.

MARGARET: And that's sane?

HYMAN: I don't know what it is! I just get the feeling sometimes that she *knows* something, something that . . . It's like she's connected to some . . . some wire that goes half around the world, some truth that other people are blind to.

MARGARET: I think you've got to get somebody on this who won't be carried away, Harry.

HYMAN: I am not carried away!

MARGARET: You really believe that Sylvia Gellburg is being threatened by these Nazis? Is that real or is it hysterical?

HYMAN: So call it hysterical, does that bring you one inch closer to what is driving that woman? It's not a word that's driving her, Margaret—she *knows* something! I don't know what it is, and she may not either—but I tell you it's real.

A moment.

MARGARET: What an interesting life you have, Harry.

Blackout.

Intermission.

Act Two

SCENE ONE

The cellist plays, music fades away.

Stanton Case is standing with hands clasped behind his back as though staring out a window. A dark mood. Gellburg enters behind him but he doesn't turn at once.

GELLBURG: Excuse me . . .

CASE, *turns:* Oh, good morning. You wanted to see me.

GELLBURG: If you have a minute I'd appreciate . . .

CASE, *as he sits:* —You don't look well, are you all right?

GELLBURG: Oh I'm fine, maybe a cold coming on . . .

Since he hasn't been invited to sit he glances at a chair then back at Case, who still leaves him hanging—and he sits on the chair's edge.

I wanted you to know how bad I feel about 611 Broadway. I'm very sorry.

CASE: Yes. Well. So it goes, I guess.

GELLBURG: I know how you had your heart set on it and I . . . I tell you the news knocked me over; they gave no sign they were talking to Allan Kershowitz or anybody else . . .

CASE: It's very disappointing—in fact, I'd already begun talking to an architect friend about renovations.

GELLBURG: Really. Well, I can't tell you how . . .

CASE: I'd gotten a real affection for that building. It certainly would have made a perfect annex. And probably a great investment too.

GELLBURG: Well, not necessarily, if Wanamaker's ever pulls out.

CASE: . . . Yes, about Wanamaker's—I should tell you— when I found out that Kershowitz had outbid us I was flabbergasted after what you'd said about the neighborhood going downhill once the store was gone— Kershowitz is no fool, I need hardly say. So I mentioned it to one of our club members who I know is related to a member of the Wanamaker board. —He tells me there has never been any discussion whatever about the company moving out; he was simply amazed at the idea.

GELLBURG: But the man at ABC . . .

CASE, *impatience showing:* ABC was left with the repair work because Wanamaker's changed to another contractor for their new boilers. It had nothing to do with the store moving out. Nothing.

GELLBURG: . . . I don't know what to say, I . . . I just . . . I'm awfully sorry . . .

CASE: Well, it's a beautiful building, let's hope Kershowitz puts it to some worthwhile use. — You have any idea what he plans to do with it?

GELLBURG: Me? Oh no, I don't really know Kershowitz.

CASE: Oh! I thought you said you knew him for years?

GELLBURG: . . . Well, I "know" him, but not . . . we're not personal friends or anything, we just met at closings a few times, and things like that. And maybe once or twice in restaurants, I think, but . . .

CASE: I see. I guess I misunderstood, I thought you were fairly close.

> *Case says no more; the full stop shoots Gellburg's anxiety way up.*

GELLBURG: I hope you're not . . . I mean I never mentioned to Kershowitz that you were interested in 611.

CASE: Mentioned? What do you mean?

GELLBURG: Nothing; just that . . . it almost sounds like I had something to do with him grabbing the building away from under you. Because I would never do a thing like that to you!

CASE: I didn't say that, did I. If I seem upset it's being screwed out of that building, and by a man whose methods I never particularly admired.

GELLBURG: Yes, that's what I mean. But I had nothing to do with Kershowitz . . .

Breaks off into silence.

CASE: But did I say you did? I'm not clear about what you wanted to say to me, or have I missed some . . . ?

GELLBURG: No-no, just that. What you just said.

CASE, *his mystification peaking:* What's the matter with you?

GELLBURG: I'm sorry. I'd like to forget the whole thing.

CASE: What's happening?

GELLBURG: Nothing. Really. I'm sorry I troubled you!

Pause. With an explosion of frustration, Case marches out. Gellburg is left open mouthed, one hand raised as though to bring back his life.

Blackout.

The cellist plays and is gone.

Sylvia in a wheelchair is listening to Eddie Cantor on the radio, singing "If You Knew Susie Like I Know Susie." She has an amused look, taps a finger to the rhythm. Her bed is nearby, on it a folded newspaper.

Hyman appears. She instantly smiles, turns off the radio, and holds a hand out to him. He comes and shakes hands.

SYLVIA, *indicating the radio:* I simply can't stand Eddie Cantor, can you?

HYMAN: Cut it out now, I heard you laughing halfway up the stairs.

SYLVIA: I know, but I can't stand him. This Crosby's the one I like. You ever hear him?

HYMAN: I can't stand these crooners—they're making ten, twenty thousand dollars a week and never spent a day in medical school. *She laughs.* Anyway, I'm an opera man.

SYLVIA: I never saw an opera. They must be hard to understand, I bet.

HYMAN: Nothing to understand—either she wants to and he doesn't or he wants to and she doesn't. *She laughs.* Either way one of them gets killed and the other one jumps off a building.

SYLVIA: I'm so glad you could come.

HYMAN, *settling into chair near the bed:*—You ready? We have to discuss something.

SYLVIA: Phillip had to go to Jersey for a zoning meeting . . .

HYMAN: Just as well—it's you I want to talk to.

SYLVIA:—There's some factory the firm owns there . . .

HYMAN: Come on, don't be nervous.

SYLVIA: . . . My back aches, will you help me onto the bed?

HYMAN: Sure.

> *He lifts her off the chair and carries her to the bed where he gently lowers her.*

There we go.

*She lies back. He brings up the blanket and covers
her legs.*

What's that perfume?

SYLVIA: Harriet found it in my drawer. I think Jerome
bought it for one of my birthdays years ago.

HYMAN: Lovely. Your hair is different.

SYLVIA, *puffs up her hair:* Harriet did it; she's loved playing
with my hair since we were kids. Did you hear all those
birds this morning?

HYMAN: Amazing, yes; a whole cloud of them shot up like
a spray in front of my horse.

SYLVIA, *partially to keep him:* You know, as a child, when we
first moved from upstate there were so many birds and
rabbits and even foxes here—Of course that was *real*
country up there; my dad had a wonderful general store,
everything from ladies' hats to horseshoes. But the winters
were just finally too cold for my mother.

HYMAN: In Coney Island we used to kill rabbits with
slingshots.

SYLVIA, *wrinkling her nose in disgust:* Why!

HYMAN, *shrugs:*—To see if we could. It was heaven for kids.

SYLVIA: I know! Brooklyn was really beautiful, wasn't it? I think people were happier then. My mother used to stand on our porch and watch us all the way to school, right across the open fields for—must have been a mile. And I would tie a clothesline around my three sisters so I wouldn't have to keep chasing after them! —I'm so glad —honestly . . . *A cozy little laugh.* I feel good every time you come.

HYMAN: Now listen to me; I've learned that these kinds of symptoms come from very deep in the mind. I would have to deal with your dreams to get any results, your deepest secret feelings, you understand? That's not my training.

SYLVIA: But when you talk to me I really feel my strength starting to come back . . .

HYMAN: You should already be having therapy to keep up your circulation.

A change in her expression, a sudden withdrawal which he notices.

You have a long life ahead of you, you don't want to live it in a wheelchair, do you? It's imperative that we get you to someone who can . . .

SYLVIA: I could tell you a dream.

HYMAN: I'm not trained to . . .

SYLVIA: I'd like to, can I?—I have the same one every night just as I'm falling asleep.

HYMAN, *forced to give way:* Well . . . all right, what is it?

SYLVIA: I'm in a street. Everything is sort of gray. And there's a crowd of people. They're packed in all around, but they're looking for me.

HYMAN: Who are they?

SYLVIA: They're Germans.

HYMAN: Sounds like those photographs in the papers.

SYLVIA, *discovering it now:* I think so, yes!

HYMAN: Does something happen?

SYLVIA: Well, I begin to run away. And the whole crowd is chasing after me. They have heavy shoes that pound on the pavement. Then just as I'm escaping around a corner a man catches me and pushes me down . . . *Breaks off.*

HYMAN: Is that the end of it?

SYLVIA: No. He gets on top of me, and begins kissing me . . . . *Breaks off.*

HYMAN: Yes?

SYLVIA: . . . And then he starts to cut off my breasts. And he raises himself up, and for a second I see the side of his face.

HYMAN: Who is it?

SYLVIA: . . . I don't know.

HYMAN: But you saw his face.

SYLVIA: I think it's Phillip. *Pause*. But how could Phillip be like . . . he was almost like one of the others?

HYMAN: I don't know. Why do you think?

SYLVIA: Would it be possible . . . because Phillip . . . I mean . . . *A little laugh* . . . he sounds sometimes like he doesn't like Jews? *Correcting*. Of course he doesn't *mean* it, but maybe in my mind it's like he's . . . *Breaks off*.

HYMAN: Like he's what. What's frightening you? *Sylvia is silent, turns away*. Sylvia?

> *Hyman tries to turn her face towards him, but she resists.*

Not Phillip, is it?

> *Sylvia turns to him, the answer is in her eyes.*

I see.

*He moves from the bed and halts, trying to weigh
this added complication. Returning to the bedside,
sits, takes her hand.*

I want to ask you a question.

She draws him to her and kisses him on the mouth.

SYLVIA: I can't help it.

She bursts into tears.

HYMAN: Oh God, Sylvia, I'm so sorry . . .

SYLVIA: Help me. Please!

HYMAN: I'm trying to.

SYLVIA: I know!

*She weeps even more deeply. With a cry filled with
her pain she embraces him desperately.*

HYMAN: Oh Sylvia, Sylvia. . . .

SYLVIA: I feel so foolish.

HYMAN: No-no. You're unhappy, not foolish.

SYLVIA: I feel like I'm losing everything, I'm being torn to
pieces. What do you want to know, I'll tell you!

*She cries into her hands. He moves, trying to make
a decision . . .*

I trust you. What do you want to ask me?

HYMAN: —Since this happened to you, have you and Phillip
had relations?

SYLVIA, *open surprise:* Relations?

HYMAN: He said you did the other night.

SYLVIA: We had *relations* the other night?

HYMAN: But that . . . well he said that by morning you'd
forgotten. Is that true?

*She is motionless, looking past him with immense
uncertainty.*

SYLVIA, *alarmed sense of rejection:* Why are you asking me that?

HYMAN: I didn't know what to make of it. . . . I guess I
still don't.

SYLVIA, *deeply embarrassed:* You mean you believe him?

HYMAN: Well . . . I didn't know what to believe.

SYLVIA: You must think I'm crazy, —to forget such a thing.

HYMAN: Oh God no!—I didn't mean anything like that . . .

SYLVIA: We haven't had relations for almost twenty years.

> *The shock pitches him into silence. Now he doesn't know what or whom to believe.*

HYMAN: Twenty . . . ? *Breaks off.*

SYLVIA: Just after Jerome was born.

HYMAN: I just ; . . I don't know what to say, Sylvia.

SYLVIA: You never heard of it before with people?

HYMAN: Yes, but not when they're as young as you.

SYLVIA: You might be surprised.

HYMAN: What was it, another woman, or what?

SYLVIA: Oh no.

HYMAN: Then what happened?

SYLVIA: I don't know, I never understood it. He just couldn't anymore.

> *She tries to read his reaction; he doesn't face her directly.*

You believe me, don't you?

HYMAN: Of course I do. But why would he invent a story like that?

SYLVIA, *incredulously:* I can't imagine. . . . Could he be trying to . . . *Breaks off.*

HYMAN: What.

SYLVIA: . . . Make you think I've gone crazy?

HYMAN: No, you mustn't believe that. I think maybe . . . you see, he mentioned my so-called reputation with women, and maybe he was just trying to look . . . I don't know—competitive. How did this start? Was there some reason?

SYLVIA: I think I made one mistake. He hadn't come near me for like—I don't remember anymore—a month maybe; and . . . I was so young . . . a man to me was so much stronger that I couldn't imagine I could . . . you know, hurt him like that.

HYMAN: Like what?

SYLVIA: Well . . . *Small laugh.* I was so stupid, I'm still ashamed of it . . . I mentioned it to my father—who loved Phillip—and he took him aside and tried to suggest a doctor. I should never have mentioned it, it was a terrible mistake, for a while I thought we'd have to have a divorce

. . . it was months before he could say good morning, he was so furious. I finally got him to go with me to Rabbi Steiner, but he just sat there like a . . . *She sighs, shakes her head.* —I don't know, I guess you just gradually give up and it closes over you like a grave. But I can't help it, I still pity him; because I know how it tortures him, it's like a snake eating into his heart. . . . I mean it's not as though he doesn't like me, he does, I know it. —Or do you think so?

HYMAN: He says you're his whole life.

She is staring, shaking her head, stunned.

SYLVIA, *with bitter irony:* His whole life! Poor Phillip.

HYMAN: I've been talking to a friend of mine at the hospital, a psychiatrist. I want your permission to bring him in; I'll call you in the morning.

SYLVIA, *instantly:* Why must you leave? I'm nervous now. Can't you talk to me a few minutes? I have some yeast cake. I'll make fresh coffee . . .

HYMAN: I'd love to stay but Margaret'll be upset with me.

SYLVIA: Oh. Well call her! Ask her to come over too.

HYMAN: No-no . . .

SYLVIA, *a sudden anxiety burst, colored by her feminine disappointment:* For God's sake, why not!

HYMAN: She thinks something's going on with us.

SYLVIA, *pleased surprise—and worriedly:* Oh!

HYMAN: I'll be in touch tomorrow . . .

SYLVIA: Couldn't you just be here when he comes. I'm nervous—please—just be here when he comes.

> *Her anxiety forces him back down on the bed. She takes his hand.*

HYMAN: You don't think he'd do something, do you?

SYLVIA: I've never known him so angry. —And I think there's also some trouble with Mr. Case. Phillip can hit, you know. *Shakes her head.* God, everything's so mixed up! *Pause. She sits there shaking her head, then lifts the newspaper.* But I don't understand—they write that the Germans are starting to pick up Jews right off the street and putting them into . . .

HYMAN, *impatience:* Now Sylvia, I told you . . .

SYLVIA: But you say they were such nice people—how could they change like this!

HYMAN: This will all pass, Sylvia! German music and literature is some of the greatest in the world; it's impossible for those people to suddenly change into thugs like this. So you ought to have more confidence, you see?—I mean in general, in life, in people.

She stares at him, becoming transformed.

HYMAN: What are you telling me? Just say what you're thinking right now.

SYLVIA, *struggling:* I . . . I . . .

HYMAN: Don't be frightened, just say it.

SYLVIA, *she has become terrified:* You.

HYMAN: Me! What about me?

SYLVIA: How could you believe I forgot we had relations!

HYMAN, *her persistent intensity unnerving him:* Now stop that! I was only trying to understand what is happening.

SYLVIA: Yes, And what? What is happening?

HYMAN, *forcefully, contained:* . . . What are you trying to tell me?

SYLVIA: Well . . . what . . .

Everything is flying apart for her; she lifts the edge
of the newspaper; the focus is clearly far wider than
the room. An unbearable anxiety . . .

What is going to become of us?

HYMAN, *indicting the paper:* —But what has Germany got to
do with . . . ?

SYLVIA, *shouting; his incomprehension dangerous:* But how can
those nice people go out and pick Jews off the street in
the middle of a big city like that, and nobody stops
them . . . ?

HYMAN: You mean *I've* changed? Is that it?

SYLVIA: I don't know . . . one minute you say you like me
and then you turn around and I'm . . .

HYMAN: Listen, I simply must call in somebody . . .

SYLVIA: No! You could help me if you believed me!

HYMAN, *his spine tingling with her fear; a shout:* I do believe
you!

SYLVIA: No!—you're not going to put me away somewhere!

HYMAN, *a horrified shout:* Now you stop being ridiculous!

SYLVIA: But . . . but what . . . what . . . *Gripping her head; his uncertainty terrifying her:* What will become of us!

HYMAN, *unnerved:* Now stop it—you are confusing two things . . . !

SYLVIA: But . . . from now on . . . you mean if a Jew walks out of his house, do they arrest him . . . ?

HYMAN: I'm telling you this won't last.

SYLVIA, *with a weird, blind, violent persistence:* But what do they do with them?

HYMAN: I don't know! I'm out of my depth! I can't help you!

SYLVIA: But why don't they run out of the country! What is the matter with those people! Don't you understand . . . ? *Screaming:* . . . This is an *emergency!* What if they kill those children! Where is Roosevelt! Where is England! Somebody should do something before they murder us all!

> *Sylvia takes a step off the edge of the bed in an hysterical attempt to reach Hyman and the power he represents. She collapses on the floor before he can catch her. Trying to rouse her from her faint . . .*

HYMAN: Sylvia? Sylvia!

Gellburg enters.

GELLBURG: What happened!

HYMAN: Run cold water on a towel!

GELLBURG: What happened!

HYMAN: Do it, goddam you!

Gellburg rushes out.

Sylvia!—oh good, that's it, keep looking at me, that's it dear, keep your eyes open . . .

> *He lifts her up onto the bed as Gellburg hurries in with a towel. Gellburg gives it to Hyman, who presses it onto her forehead and back of her neck.*

There we are, that's better, how do you feel? Can you speak? You want to sit up? Come.

> *He helps her to sit up. She looks around and then at Gellburg.*

GELLBURG, *to Hyman:* Did *she* call *you*?

HYMAN, *hesitates; and in an angry tone:* . . . Well no, to tell the truth.

GELLBURG: Then what are you doing here?

HYMAN: I stopped by, I was worried about her.

GELLBURG: You were worried about her. Why were you worried about her?

HYMAN, *anger is suddenly sweeping him:* Because she is desperate to be loved.

GELLBURG, *off guard, astonished:* You don't say!

HYMAN: Yes, I do say. *To her:* I want you to try to move your legs. Try it.

> *She tries; nothing happens.*

I'll be at home if you need me; don't be afraid to call anytime. We'll talk about this more tomorrow. Good night.

SYLVIA, *faintly, afraid:* Good night.

> *Hyman gives Gellburg a quick, outraged glance, Hyman leaves.*

GELLBURG, *reaching for his authority:* That's some attitude he's got, ordering me around like that. I'm going to see about getting somebody else tomorrow. Jersey seems to get further and further away, I'm exhausted.

SYLVIA: I almost started walking.

GELLBURG: What are you talking about?

SYLVIA: For a minute. I don't know what happened, my strength, it started to come back.

GELLBURG: I knew it! I told you you could! Try it again, come.

SYLVIA, *she tries to raise her legs:* I can't now.

GELLBURG: Why not! Come, this is wonderful . . . ! *Reaches for her.*

SYLVIA: Phillip, listen . . . I don't want to change, I want Hyman.

GELLBURG, *his purse-mouthed grin:* What's so good about him?—you're still laying there, practically dead to the world.

SYLVIA: He helped me get up, I don't know why. I feel he can get me walking again.

GELLBURG: Why does it have to be him?

SYLVIA: Because I can talk to him! I want *him. An outburst:* And I don't want to discuss it again!

GELLBURG: Well we'll see.

SYLVIA: We will not see!

GELLBURG: What's this tone of voice?

SYLVIA, *trembling out of control:* It's a Jewish woman's tone of voice!

GELLBURG: A Jewish woman . . . ! What are you talking about, are you crazy?

SYLVIA: Don't you call me crazy, Phillip! I'm talking about it! They are smashing windows and beating children! I am talking about it! *Screams at him:* I am talking about it, Phillip!

> She grips her head in her confusion. He is stock still; horrified, fearful.

GELLBURG: What . . . "beating children"?

SYLVIA: Never mind. Don't sleep with me again.

GELLBURG: How can you say that to me?

SYLVIA: I can't bear it. You give me terrible dreams. I'm sorry, Phillip. Maybe in a while but not now.

GELLBURG: Sylvia, you will kill me if we can't be together . . .

SYLVIA: You told him we had relations?

GELLBURG, *beginning to weep:* Don't, Sylvia . . . !

SYLVIA: You little liar!—you want him to think I'm crazy? Is that it? *Now she breaks into weeping.*

GELLBURG: No! It just . . . it came out, I didn't know what I was saying!

SYLVIA: *That I forgot we had relations?! Phillip?*

GELLBURG: Stop that! Don't say anymore.

SYLVIA: I'm going to say anything I want to.

GELLBURG, *weeping:* You will kill me . . . !

They are silent for a moment.

SYLVIA: What I did with my life! Out of ignorance. Out of not wanting to shame you in front of other people. A whole life. Gave it away like a couple of pennies—I took better care of my shoes. *Turns to him.* —You want to talk to me about it now? Take me seriously, Phillip. What happened? I know it's all you ever thought about, isn't that true? *What happened?* Just so I'll know.

A long pause.

GELLBURG: I'm ashamed to mention it. It's ridiculous.

SYLVIA: What are you talking about?

GELLBURG: But I was ignorant, I couldn't help myself. —
When you said you wanted to go back to the firm.

SYLVIA: What are you talking about?—When?

GELLBURG: When you had Jerome . . . and suddenly you
didn't want to keep the house anymore.

SYLVIA: And? —You didn't want me to go back to business,
so I didn't.

He doesn't speak; her rage an inch below.

Well what? I didn't, did I?

GELLBURG: You held it against me, having to stay home,
you know you did. You've probably forgotten, but not a
day passed, not a person could come into this house that
you didn't keep saying how wonderful and interesting it
used to be for you in business. You never forgave me,
Sylvia.

She evades his gaze.

So whenever I . . . when I started to touch you, I felt
that.

SYLVIA: You felt what?

GELLBURG: That you didn't want me to be the man here.
And then, on top of that when you didn't want any more

children . . . everything inside me just dried up. And maybe it was also that to me it was a miracle you ever married me in the first place.

SYLVIA: You mean your face?

He turns slightly.

What have you got against your face? A Jew can have a Jewish face.

Pause.

GELLBURG: I can't help my thoughts, nobody can. . . . I admit it was a mistake, I tried a hundred times to talk to you, but I couldn't. I kept waiting for myself to change. Or you. And then we got to where it didn't seem to matter anymore. So I left it. that way. And I couldn't change anything anymore.

Pause.

SYLVIA: This is a whole life we're talking about.

GELLBURG: But couldn't we . . . if I taught you to drive and you could go anywhere you liked. . . . Or maybe you could find a position you liked . . . ?

She is staring ahead.

We have to sleep together.

SYLVIA: No.

Gellburg drops to his knees beside the bed, his arms spread awkwardly over her covered body.

GELLBURG: How can this be?

She is motionless.

Sylvia? *Pause.* Do you want to kill me?

She is staring ahead, he is weeping and shouting.

Is that it! Speak to me!

Sylvia's face is blank, unreadable. He buries his face in the covers, weeping helplessly. She at last reaches out in pity toward the top of his head, and as her hand almost touches . . .

Blackout.

Case's office. Gellburg is seated alone. Case enters, shuffling through a handful of mail. Gellburg has gotten to his feet. Case's manner is cold; barely glances up from his mail.

CASE: Good morning, Gellburg.

GELLBURG: Good morning, Mr. Case.

CASE: I understand you wish to see me.

GELLBURG: There was just something I felt I should say.

CASE: Certainly. *He goes to a chair and sits.* Yes?

GELLBURG: It's just that I would never in this world do anything against you or Brooklyn Guarantee. I don't have to tell you, it's the only place I've ever worked in my life. My whole life is here. I'm more proud of this company than almost anything except my own son. What I'm try-ing to say is that this whole business with Wanamaker's was only because I didn't want to leave a stone unturned. Two or three years from now I didn't want you waking up one morning and Wanamaker's is gone and there you

are paying New York taxes on a building in the middle
of a dying neighborhood.

Case lets him hang there. He begins getting flustered.

Frankly, I don't even remember what this whole thing
was about. I feel I've lost some of your confidence, and
it's . . . well, it's unfair, I feel.

CASE: I understand.

GELLBURG, *he waits, but that's it:* But . . . but don't you
believe me?

CASE: I think I do.

GELLBURG: But . . . you seem to be . . . you don't seem . . .

CASE: The fact remains that I've lost the building.

GELLBURG: But are you . . . I mean you're not still thinking
that I had something going on with Allan Kershowitz,
are you?

CASE: Put it this way—I hope as time goes on that my old
confidence will return. That's about as far as I can go, and
I don't think you can blame me, can you. *He stands.*

GELLBURG, *despite himself his voice rises:* But how can I work
if you're this way? You have to trust a man, don't you?

CASE, *begins to indicate he must leave:* I'll have to ask you to . . .

GELLBURG, *shouting:* I don't deserve this! You can't do this to me! It's not fair, Mr. Case, I had nothing to do with Allan Kershowitz! I hardly know the man! And the little I do know I don't even like him, I'd certainly never get into a deal with him, for God's sake! This is . . . this whole thing is . . . *Exploding:* I don't understand it, what is happening, what the hell is happening, what have I got to do with Allan Kershowitz, just because he's also a Jew?

CASE, *incredulously and angering:* What? What on earth are you talking about!

GELLBURG: Excuse me. I didn't mean that.

CASE: I don't understand . . . how could you say a thing like that!

GELLBURG: Please. I don't feel well, excuse me . . .

CASE, *his resentment mounting:* But how could you say such a thing! It's an outrage, Gellburg!

> *Gellburg takes a step to leave and goes to his knees, clutching his chest, trying to breathe, his face reddening.*

CASE: What is it? Gellburg? *He springs up and goes to the periphery.* Call an ambulance! Hurry, for God's sake! *He*

rushes out, shouting: Quick, get a doctor! It's Gellburg!
Gellburg has collapsed!

> *Gellburg remains on his hands and knees trying to*
> *keep from falling over, gasping.*

> *Blackout.*

SCENE FOUR

Sylvia in wheelchair, Margaret and Harriet seated on either side of her. Sylvia is sipping a cup of cocoa.

HARRIET: He's really amazing, after such an attack.

MARGARET: The heart is a muscle; muscles can recover sometimes.

HARRIET: I still can't understand how they let him out of the hospital so soon.

MARGARET: He has a will of iron. But it may be just as well for him here.

SYLVIA: He wants to die here.

MARGARET: No one can know, he can live a long time.

SYLVIA, *handing her the cup:* Thanks. I haven't drunk cocoa in years.

MARGARET: I find it soothes the nerves.

SYLVIA, *with a slight ironical edge:* He wants to be here so we
can have a talk, that's what it is. *Shakes her head.* How
stupid it all is; you keep putting everything off like you're
going to live a thousand years. But we're like those little
flies—born in the morning, fly around for a day till it gets
dark—and bye-bye.

HARRIET: Well, it takes time to learn things.

SYLVIA: There's nothing I know now that I didn't know
twenty years ago. I just didn't say it. *Grasping the chair
wheels.* Help me! I want to go to him.

MARGARET: Wait till Harry says it's all right.

HARRIET: Sylvia, please—let the doctor decide.

MARGARET: I hope you're not blaming yourself.

HARRIET: It could happen to anybody—*To Margaret.* Our
father, for instance—laid down for his nap one afternoon
and never woke up. *To Sylvia.* Remember?

SYLVIA, *a wan smile, nods:* He was the same way all his life
—never wanted to trouble anybody.

HARRIET: And just the day before he went and bought a
new bathing suit. And an amber holder for his cigar. *To
Sylvia*—She's right, you mustn't start blaming yourself.

SYLVIA, *a shrug:* What's the difference? *Sighs tiredly—stares.*
Basically to Margaret. The trouble, you see—was that Phillip always thought he was supposed to be the Rock of
Gibraltar. Like nothing could ever bother him. Suppos-
edly. But I knew a couple of months after we got married
that he . . . he was making it all up. In fact, I thought I
was stronger than him. But what can you do? You swal-
low it and make believe you're weaker. And after a while
you can't find a true word to put in your mouth. And
now I end up useless to him . . . *starting to weep,* just when
he needs me!

HARRIET, *distressed, stands:* I'm making a gorgeous pot roast,
can I bring some over?

SYLVIA: Thanks, Flora's going to cook something.

HARRIET: I'll call you later, try to rest. *Moves to leave, halts,*
unable to hold back. I refuse to believe that you're blaming
yourself for this. How can people start saying what they
know?—there wouldn't be two marriages left in Brooklyn! *Nearly overcome.* It's ridiculous!—you're the best wife
he could have had!—better! *She hurries out. Pause.*

MARGARET: I worked in the pediatric ward for a couple of
years. And sometimes we'd have thirty or forty babies in
there at the same time. A day or two old and they've
already got a personality; this one lays there, stiff as a
mummy . . . *mimes a mummy, hands closed in fists,* a regular
banker. The next one is throwing himself all over the
place . . . *wildly flinging her arms,* happy as a young horse.

The next one is Miss Dreary, already worried about her hemline drooping. And how could it be otherwise—each one has twenty thousand years of the human race backed up behind him . . . and you expect to change him?

SYLVIA: So what does that mean? How do you live?

MARGARET: You draw your cards face down; you turn them over and do your best with the hand you got. What else is there, my dear? What else can there be?

SYLVIA, *staring ahead:* . . . Wishing, I guess . . . that it had been otherwise. Help me! *Starts the chair rolling.* I want to go to him.

MARGARET: Wait. I'll ask Harry if it's all right. *Backing away.* Wait, okay? I'll be right back.

> *She turns and exits. Alone, Sylvia brings both hands pressed together up to her lips in a sort of prayer, and closes her eyes.*

Blackout.

The cellist plays, the music falls away.

Gellburg's bedroom. He is in bed. Hyman is putting his stethoscope back into his bag, and sits on a chair beside the bed.

HYMAN: I can only tell you again, Phillip,—you belong in the hospital.

GELLBURG: Please don't argue about it anymore! I couldn't stand it there, it smells like a zoo; and to lay in a bed where some stranger died . . . I hate it. If I'm going out I'll go from here. And I don't want to leave Sylvia.

HYMAN: I'm trying to help you. *Chuckles.* And I'm going to go on trying even if it kills both of us.

GELLBURG: I appreciate that. I mean it. You're a good man.

HYMAN: You're lucky I know that. The nurse should be here around six.

GELLBURG: I'm wondering if I need her—I think the pain is practically gone.

HYMAN: I want her here overnight.

GELLBURG: I . . . I want to tell you something; when I collapsed . . . it was like an explosion went off in my head, like a tremendous white light. It sounds funny but I felt a . . . happiness . . . that funny? Like I suddenly had something to tell her that would change everything, and we would go back to how it was when we started out together. I couldn't wait to tell it to her . . . and now I can't remember what it was. *Anguished, a rushed quality; suddenly near tears.* God, I always thought there'd be time to get to the bottom of myself!

HYMAN: You might have years, nobody can predict.

GELLBURG: It's unbelievable—the first time since I was twenty I don't have a job. I just can't believe it.

HYMAN: You sure? Maybe you can clear it up with your boss when you go back.

GELLBURG: How can I go back? He made a fool of me. It's infuriating. I tell you—I never wanted to see it this way but he goes sailing around on the ocean and meanwhile I'm foreclosing Brooklyn for them. That's what it boils down to. You got some lousy rotten job to do, get Gellburg, send in the Yid. Close down a business, throw somebody out of his home. . . . And now to accuse me . . .

HYMAN: But is all this news to you? That's the system, isn't it?

GELLBURG: But to accuse me of double-crossing the *company*! That is absolutely unfair . . . it was like a hammer between the eyes. I mean to me Brooklyn Guarantee— for God's sake, Brooklyn Guarantee was like . . . like . . .

HYMAN: You're getting too excited, Phillip . . . come on now. *Changing the subject:* —I understand your son is coming back from the Philippines.

GELLBURG, *he catches his breath for a moment:* . . . She show you his telegram? He's trying to make it here by Monday. *Scared eyes and a grin.* Or will I last till Monday?

HYMAN: You've got to start thinking about more positive things—seriously, your system needs a rest.

GELLBURG: Who's that talking?

HYMAN, *indicating upstage:* I asked Margaret to sit with your wife for a while, they're in your son's bedroom.

GELLBURG: Do you always take so much trouble?

HYMAN: I like Sylvia.

GELLBURG, *his little grin:* I know . . . I didn't think it was for my sake.

HYMAN: You're not so bad. I have to get back to my office now.

GELLBURG: Please if you have a few minutes, I'd appreciate it. *Almost holding his breath.* Tell me——the thing she's so afraid of . . . is me isn't it?

HYMAN: Well . . . among other things.

GELLBURG, *shock:* It's me?

HYMAN: I think so . . . partly.

Gellburg presses his fingers against his eyes to regain control.

GELLBURG: How could she be frightened of me! I worship her! *Quickly controlling:* How could everything turn out to be the opposite——I made my son in this bed and now I'm dying in it . . . *Breaks off, downing a cry.* My thoughts keep flying around——everything from years ago keeps coming back like it was last week. Like the day we bought this bed. Abraham & Straus. It was so sunny and beautiful. I took the whole day off. (God, it's almost twenty-five years ago!) . . . Then we had a soda at Schrafft's——of course they don't hire Jews but the chocolate ice cream is the best. Then we went over to Orchard Street for bargains. Bought our first pots and sheets, blankets, pillowcases. The street was full of pushcarts and men with long beards like a hundred years ago. It's funny, I felt so at home and happy there that day, a street full of Jews, one Moses after another. But they all turned to watch her go by, those fakers. She was a knockout; sometimes walking down a street I couldn't believe I was married to her. Listen . . . *Breaks off, with some diffidence:* You're an educated man, I only went to high school—I wish we could talk about the Jews.

HYMAN: I never studied the history, if that's what you . . .

GELLBURG: . . . I don't know where I am . . .

HYMAN: You mean as a Jew?

GELLBURG: Do you think about it much? I never . . . for instance, a Jew in love with horses is something I never heard of.

HYMAN: My grandfather in Odessa was a horse dealer.

GELLBURG: You don't say! I wouldn't know you were Jewish except for your name.

HYMAN: I have cousins up near Syracuse who're still in the business—they break horses. You know there are Chinese Jews.

GELLBURG: I heard of that! And they look Chinese?

HYMAN: They are Chinese. They'd probably say you don't look Jewish.

GELLBURG: Ha! That's funny. *His laugh disappears; he stares.*
Why is it so hard to be a Jew?

HYMAN: It's hard to be anything.

GELLBURG: No, it's different for them. Being a Jew is a full-
time job. Except you don't think about it much, do you.
—Like when you're on your horse, or . . .

HYMAN: It's not an obsession for me . . .

GELLBURG: But how'd you come to marry a shiksa?

HYMAN: We were thrown together when I was interning,
and we got very close, and . . . well she was a good
partner, she helped me, and still does. And I loved her.

GELLBURG: —a Jewish woman couldn't help you?

HYMAN: Sure. But it just didn't happen.

GELLBURG: It wasn't so you wouldn't seem Jewish.

HYMAN, *coldly:* I never pretended I wasn't Jewish.

GELLBURG, *almost shaking with some fear:* Look, don't be mad,
I'm only trying to figure out . . .

HYMAN, *sensing the underlying hostility:* What are you driving
at, I don't understand this whole conversation.

GELLBURG: Hyman . . . Help me! I've never been so afraid in my life.

HYMAN: If you're alive you're afraid; we're born afraid—a newborn baby is not a picture of confidence; but how you deal with fear, that's what counts. I don't think you dealt with it very well.

GELLBURG: Why? How did I deal with it?

HYMAN: I think you tried to disappear into the goyim.

GELLBURG: . . . You believe in God?

HYMAN: I'm a socialist. I think we're at the end of religion.

GELLBURG: You mean everybody working for the government.

HYMAN: It's the only future that makes any rational sense.

GELLBURG: God forbid. But how can there be Jews if there's no God?

HYMAN: Oh, they'll find something to worship. The Christians will too—maybe different brands of ketchup.

GELLBURG, laughs: Boy, the things you come out with sometimes . . . !

HYMAN: —Some day we're all going to look like a lot of monkeys running around trying to figure out a coconut.

GELLBURG: She believes in you, Hyman . . . I want you to tell her—tell her I'm going to change. She has no right to be so frightened. Of me or anything else. They will never destroy us. When the last Jew dies, the light of the world will go out. She has to understand that—those Germans are shooting at the sun!

HYMAN: Be quiet.

GELLBURG: I want my wife back. I want her back before something happens. I feel like there's nothing inside me, I feel empty. I want her back.

HYMAN: Phillip, what can I do about that?

GELLBURG: Never mind . . . since you started coming around . . . in those boots . . . like some kind of horseback rider . . . ?

HYMAN: What the hell are you talking about!

GELLBURG: Since you came around she looks down at me like a miserable piece of shit!

HYMAN: Phillip . . .

GELLBURG: Don't "Phillip" me, just stop it!

HYMAN: Don't scream at me Phillip, you know how to get your wife back! . . . don't tell me there's a mystery to that!

GELLBURG: She actually told you that I . . .

HYMAN: It came out while we were talking. It was bound to sooner or later, wasn't it?

GELLBURG, *gritting his teeth:* I never told this to anyone . . . but years ago when I used to make love to her, I would almost feel like a small baby on top of her, like she was giving me birth. That's some idea? In bed next to me she was like a . . . a marble god. I worshipped her, Hyman, from the day I laid eyes on her.

HYMAN: I'm sorry for you Phillip.

GELLBURG: How can she be so afraid of me? Tell me the truth.

HYMAN: I don't know; maybe, for one thing . . . these remarks you're always making about Jews.

GELLBURG: What remarks?

HYMAN: Like not wanting to be mistaken for Goldberg.

GELLBURG: So I'm a Nazi? Is Gellburg Goldberg? It's not, is it?

HYMAN: No, but continually making the point is kind of . . .

GELLBURG: Kind of what? What is kind of? Why don't you say the truth?

HYMAN: All right, you want the truth? Do you? Look in the mirror sometime!

GELLBURG: . . . In the mirror!

HYMAN: You hate yourself, that's what's scaring her to death. That's my opinion. How it's possible I don't know, but I think you helped paralyze her with this "Jew, Jew, Jew" coming out of your mouth and the same time she reads it in the paper and it's coming out of the radio day and night? You wanted to know what I think . . . that's what I think.

GELLBURG: But there are some days I feel like going and sitting in the *schul* with the old men and pulling the *talles* over my head and be a full-time Jew the rest of my life. With the sidelocks and the black hat, and settle it once and for all. And other times . . . yes, I could almost kill them. They infuriate me. I am ashamed of them and that I look like them. *Gasping again:* —Why must we be different? Why is it? What is it for?

HYMAN: And supposing it turns out that we're *not* different, who are you going to blame then?

GELLBURG: What are you talking about?

HYMAN: I'm talking about all this grinding and screaming that's going on inside you—you're wearing yourself out for nothing, Phillip, absolutely nothing! —I'll tell you a secret—I have all kinds coming into my office, and there's not one of them who one way or another is not persecuted. Yes. *Everybody's* persecuted. The poor by the rich, the rich by the poor, the black by the white, the white by the black, the men by the women, the women by the men, the Catholics by the Protestants, the Protestants by the Catholics—and of course all of them by the Jews. Everybody's persecuted—sometimes I wonder, maybe that's what holds this country together! And what's really amazing is that you can't find anybody who's persecuting anybody else.

GELLBURG: So you mean there's no Hitler?

HYMAN: Hitler? Hitler is the perfect example of the persecuted man! I've heard him—he kvetches like an elephant was standing on his pecker! They've turned that whole beautiful country into one gigantic kvetch! *Takes his bag.* The nurse'll be here soon.

GELLBURG: So what's the solution?

HYMAN: I don't see any. Except the mirror. But nobody's going to look at himself and ask what am *I* doing—you might as well tell him to take a seat in the hottest part of hell. Forgive her, Phillip, is all I really know to tell you. *Grins*: But that's the easy part—I speak from experience.

GELLBURG: What's the hard part?

HYMAN: To forgive yourself, I guess. And the Jews. And while you're at it, you can throw in the goyim. Best thing for the heart you know.

> *Hyman exits. Gellburg is left alone, staring into space. Sylvia enters, Margaret pushing the chair.*

MARGARET: I'll leave you now, Sylvia.

SYLVIA: Thanks for sitting with me.

GELLBURG, *a little wave of the hand:* Thank you Mrs. Hyman!

MARGARET: I think your color's coming back a little.

GELLBURG: Well, I've been running around the block.

MARGARET, *a burst of laughter and shaking her finger at him:* I always knew there was a sense of humor somewhere inside that black suit!

GELLBURG: Yes, well . . . I finally got the joke.

MARGARET, *laughs, and to Sylvia:* I'll try to look in tomorrow. *To both:* Good-bye!

> *Margaret exits.*

> *A silence between them grows self-conscious.*

GELLBURG: You all right in that room?

SYLVIA: It's better this way, we'll both get more rest. You all right?

GELLBURG: I want to apologize.

SYLVIA: I'm not blaming you, Phillip. The years I wasted I know I threw away myself. I think I always knew I was doing it but I couldn't stop it.

GELLBURG: If only you could believe I never meant you harm, it would . . .

SYLVIA: I believe you. But I have to tell you something. When I said not to sleep with me . . .

GELLBURG: I know . . .

SYLVIA, *nervously sharp:* You don't know!—I'm trying to tell you something! *Containing herself:* For some reason I keep thinking of how I used to be; remember my parents' house, how full of love it always was? Nobody was ever afraid of anything. But with us, Phillip, wherever I looked there was something to be suspicious about, somebody who was going to take advantage or God knows what. I've been tip-toeing around my life for thirty years and I'm not going to pretend—I hate it all now. Everything I did is stupid and ridiculous. I can't find myself in my life.

She hits her legs.

Or in this now, this thing that can't even walk. I'm not this thing. And it has me. It has me and will never let me go.

She weeps.

GELLBURG: Sshh! I understand. I wasn't telling you the truth. I always tried to seem otherwise, but I've been more afraid than I looked.

SYLVIA: Afraid of what?

GELLBURG: Everything. Of Germany. Mr. Case. Of what could happen to us here. I think I was more afraid than you are, a hundred times more! And meantime there are Chinese Jews, for God's sake.

SYLVIA: What do you mean?

GELLBURG: They're *Chinese!*—and here I spend a lifetime looking in the mirror at my face!—Why we're different I will never understand but to live so afraid, I don't want that anymore. I tell you, if I live I have to try to change myself.—Sylvia, my darling Sylvia, I'm asking you not to blame me anymore. I feel I did this to you! That's the knife in my heart.

Gellburg's breathing begins to labor.

SYLVIA, *alarmed:* Phillip!

GELLBURG: God almighty, Sylvia forgive me!

*A paroxysm forces Gellburg up to a nearly sitting
position, agony on his face.*

SYLVIA: Wait! Phillip!

*Struggling to break free of the chair's support, she
starts pressing down on the chair arms.*

There's nothing to blame! There's nothing to blame!

*Gellburg falls back, unconscious. She struggles to bal-
ance herself on her legs and takes a faltering step
toward her husband.*

Wait, wait . . . Phillip, Phillip!

*Astounded, charged with hope yet with a certain in-
ward seeing, she looks down at her legs, only now
aware that she has risen to her feet.*

Lights fade.

THE END.